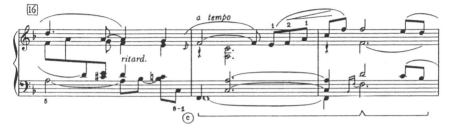

ⓒ The first edition has 🐦 at each of these places, but no release is shown.

PIANO LESSONS

Also by Noah Adams

Saint Croix Notes: River Mornings, Radio Nights

Noah Adams on All Things Considered: *A Radio Journal*

PIANO LESSONS

Music, Love, & True Adventures

NOAH ADAMS

Delacorte Press

Published by
Delacorte Press
Bantam Doubleday Dell Publishing Group, Inc.
1540 Broadway
New York, New York 10036

Library of Congress Cataloging in Publication Data

Adams, Noah.
    Piano lessons : music, love, & true adventures / Noah Adams.
      p.   cm.
    Includes bibliographical references (p.   ).
    ISBN 0-385-31404-3
    1. Adams, Noah. 2. Pianists—United States—Biography.
I. Title.
ML417.A23A3   1996
786.2′092—dc20
  [B]   95-31761
                                 CIP
                                 MN

Designed by Jeffrey L. Ward

Manufactured in the United States of America
Published simultaneously in Canada

April 1996

10 9 8 7 6 5 4 3 2 1

BVG

For all who would play

[and for Stanley Joseph, who certainly did]

CONTENTS

CONTENTS

Acknowledgments

THANKS TO ELLEN WEISS OF *ALL THINGS CONSIDERED* FOR a few extra piano weeks off and for not minding my occasional inattention to the daily news. Thanks also to Melissa Block and Paul Lewis for reading an early draft of the manuscript and to Neenah Ellis for fact-checking help. My appreciation as well to the MacDowell Colony in Peterborough, New Hampshire, to my agent, Jonathon Lazear, and to Steve Ross at Delacorte Press, who will someday *be* a piano player.

Each moment I live, I must think
where to place my fingers, and press
them down with no confidence of
hearing a chord.

> —John Updike
> from the story
> "The Music School"

Introduction

PLAY THE FIRST NOTE RIGHT. THE MORNING—SUNRISE, eleven degrees, wind dancing across overnight snow— waits for a perfectly struck single note.

"Träumerei," by Robert Schumann, begins with middle C (a year ago this was the only note I could find on the piano). The next note is an F in the right hand joined by an F in the bass; then a cautious chord in both hands and five ascending treble notes lift the song into the air. There's a quick, deep pulse in my throat and a fast breath, and I'm smiling, watching the page, trying to stay up with the melody.

I've come to a quiet place in southern New Hampshire to write about the past year and my involvement with the piano. Often in the early mornings I'll bring a thermos of coffee and my music here to the library, a small stone building at the edge of a field. I'll unlock the heavy front door, turn up the thermostat, take the cover off the piano—it's a Steinway B Model, made in Hamburg, West Germany, in 1962—and play for an hour or so. The ivory-topped keys are cold at first, and so are my hands. I start with exercises, playing in unison an octave apart, up and down the keyboard. Sometimes I notice a tremble, a shaking in the last two fingers of my left hand. In the morning light, though, my hands look young. (The backs of my hands have always seemed old, wrinkled; once at a grade-school Halloween party someone recognized me by my hands, not covered by my ghost costume.)

Then I'll practice "Träumerei." This piece—only two pages, three minutes long—is teaching me piano. There are technical knots to be worked loose, clues to mysteries hiding in the notation. I would be happy to play it several thousand times.

Vladimir Horowitz used to play "Träumerei" as an encore; he said it was a masterpiece. Robert Schumann was only twenty-seven when he wrote the music, and I have the feeling he finished it in a couple of hours, one afternoon. It seems a passionate time in his life; in a letter to a friend he said: "I feel I could almost burst with music—I simply have to compose." Schumann was in love with Clara Wieck, a young piano virtuoso. Her father disapproved and had taken Clara away on a recital tour. "Träumerei" is one of thirteen short pieces in a collection called *Kinderszenen (Scenes from Childhood)*. As Schumann put it, the songs were "reminiscences of a grown-up for grown-ups." (*Träumerei* translates as "reverie.") And he said in a letter to Clara, "You will enjoy them—though you will have to forget that you are a virtuoso . . . they're all easy to carry off." Schumann told Clara these pieces were "peaceful, tender and happy, like our future."

I can see him at his writing desk, and piano, in Leipzig. Excited, dreaming of Clara, his own career as a pianist doomed by a hand injury but by this time knowing that he could be a composer. Twenty-seven years old! Not ten years before, he was a college student, writing home to his mother asking for more money.

> *I am living like a dog. My hair is yards long and I want to get it cut, but I can't spare a penny. My piano is terribly out of tune but I can't afford to get a tuner. I haven't even got the money for a pistol to shoot myself with. . . .*
>
> Your miserable son,
> Robert Schumann

He loved drinking and cigars. It seems a historical rumor that he had syphilis. He was probably manic-depressive early as an adult, and later suicidal. He *heard* hallucinations. "He is in terrible agony," his wife, Clara, wrote in her diary. "Every sound he hears turns to music. Music played on glorious sounding instruments, he says, more beautiful than any music ever heard on earth. It utterly exhausts him."

Robert Schumann died in a mental asylum, at age forty-six. He starved himself to death. Clara did see him, once, as he was dying, but he was kept away from his family for two years. A visitor once peered through an opening in his door and saw him playing a piano, lost apparently in improvisation, but playing music that made no sense. As I sit at this piano in New Hampshire, I have outlived Schumann by six years.

I bought a piece of granite the other day, from a monument company across the road from the town cemetery. I gave the guy twenty dollars and put the "surveyor's post" in the back of my station wagon. Granite is heavy; I don't know why I was surprised. The post is two feet high and about four inches square, with two rough sides and two that have been trimmed smooth. I don't think I'll have to explain this to Neenah, my wife. That the permanence of the granite appeals to me, that the years going by so quickly need marking, with piano lessons and stone. "Oh, that's a good thing to bring back from New Hampshire," she'll say.

I noticed the posts when I was out running, before lunchtime, along the town streets and then out a bit into the country. You'd see them at the corner of a yard by the driveway. The older houses would have large granite posts out front, sometimes chiseled with a street number. And you'd see the odd stub of a post marking a boundary, the stone weathered and chipped by lawn mowers or snow blades. When Robert Schumann died, in 1856, granite buildings in this town had been standing for ten years.

There's not quite enough light on the piano and I have to squint to see the faint marking "a tempo" at the end of the first eight measures of "Träumerei," meaning a return to normal after the slowing of "ritard." I've repeated these measures, with some parts a bit softer, taking a teacher's advice: If you don't have something different to say in the repeat, why bother playing it? The tricky middle section waits, a difficult passage in the bass clef, a climb to the treble for another. I remember to relax my shoulders and try to make my hands heavier and pretend these are my favorite parts. It's whistling past the graveyard—and it almost works. I play one chord that's not sounded clearly, I forget to hold an A in the left hand, my foot hits the sustain pedal to slur over a mistake in fingering, but the notes are correct, and there's still a singing quality to the melody.

It's a lovely-sounding piano. A seven-foot grand, shiny mahogany. I have the top all the way up, as you would for a concert. It is my dream, when I touch the keys, to *release* the notes. It is music waiting there, and for me it is as real as the blown snow against the windows, and the evening's quarter moon rising through a cold fog, or the stories told of wolves that lived on nearby Mount Monadnock, sheltering in the red oak trees. Robert Frost wrote about valleys and mountains like these and once of a farmer whose land was so high up that his neighbors could watch the light of his lantern as he went about his chores.

I can feel my shoulders tightening again as I get close to the end of "Träumerei." I try to sway a bit on the piano bench, and I sing out loud with the phrases. The opening theme returns, starting with middle C. Then up to a solid, proud seven-note chord and (ritardando) a stately, quiet finish. There is a fermata over the final chord: a black dot with a half circle on top. A "bird's eye" musicians call it. The symbol means, "Hold it as long as you want to, you've earned it." And there's a pedal marking at the bottom; the pedal goes down *as* you play the chord so all the other Fs and As on the keyboard sound in sympathetic resonance.

I gently release the pedal and the final, whispering tones are dampened and lost in the warming rush of air from the furnace. There's a small puddle of water from my boots on the flagstone floor. The sunlight has now reached the trees at the edge of the field.

On the shelves around the piano are bound sets of sheet music, Strauss and Wagner, Mozart. Schumann's works are here, in several volumes. I can play one of his songs, imperfectly (I've surely played "Träumerei" more times than he did), and it's really the only piece of music that I've learned. It was an unanticipated, almost reckless year. I was at first surprised and delighted by the piano, then daunted, then discouraged. By the fall I had almost given up. By October's end, though, I was learning. In November and December, as now, I wanted to spend all my time practicing.

I'll take the granite post back home to Washington and, when the weather warms, dig a hole for it at the edge of the garden. You could set your coffee cup on top of the post, or a trowel.

I'll play the piano for my wife, early in the morning, and tell her about my adventures.

N. D. A.
The MacDowell Colony
Peterborough, New Hampshire

THE INVESTMENT

BY ROBERT FROST

Over back where they speak of life as staying
("You couldn't call it living, for it ain't"),
There was an old, old house renewed with paint,
And in it a piano loudly playing.

Out in the plowed ground in the cold a digger,
Among the unearthed potatoes standing still,
Was counting winter dinners, one a hill,
With half an ear to the piano's vigor.

All that piano and new paint back there,
Was it some money suddenly come into?
Or some extravagance young love had been to?
Or old love on an impulse not to care—

Not to sink under being man and wife,
But get some color and music out of life?

JANUARY

> *Why does a fifty-one-year-old man decide he has to have a piano?*

SUNSHINE ON NEW YEAR'S DAY, AND OUR CELEBRATION starts with the radio: a live broadcast from Vienna. There is an expectant hush, and then the shimmering French horns begin "On the Beautiful Blue Danube." We've had a quiet morning listening to Strauss, making pancakes for breakfast, reading the papers, trying to straighten up the room we use as an office. When the encore starts, the "Blue Danube," Neenah comes in from the kitchen. She's wearing a red plaid robe, she's holding Sally, the cat, in her arms, and she's waltzing. The dogs bounce around happily, pretending they understand the occasion. Lorin Maazel leads the Vienna Philharmonic Orchestra on into the song, and I can feel

1

the promise of the morning and the year ahead tingling through my body.

And there's a question to be answered, a daily, perplexing thought. Should I buy a piano?

My best memories often resonate with music. And two scenes have stayed especially vibrant. The first one comes back every time I hear a certain low piano note.

It is summer and I am fifteen. The windows of the old brick building are open, and I can hear the music pounding into the night air as we drive up and park the car and drink some more beer for courage and walk up to the front steps. I'm grinning, bouncing with the piano beat—an *extreme* boogie-woogie. We go inside where the jukebox is turned all the way up and Jerry Lee Lewis is singing "Whole Lot of Shakin' Going On." My friends and I stand in the darkness against the wall, watching the dancers, listening. I've never heard music like this; I feel as if I'm standing *inside* the piano as the bass notes roll up the keyboard and rip back down. The treble notes spill from the top in terrifying slides. And Jerry Lee Lewis sings, "You can shake it one time for me . . . all you gotta do, honey, is kinda stand in one spot and just wiggle around a little bit." I watch one of the girls from my school moving her hips inside a tight skirt. She's leaning back with her eyes closed, short blond hair shining, her small breasts bouncing lightly with the music. The song ends and then starts over again. I stay by the wall. We're football players and don't dance; we just walk in and look cool. But I wonder—achingly—about the courage it would take to go ahead and try it. And then what *could* happen with the girl?

Thirty years later, in 1987, I fell in love with the piano on the stage of the World Theater in St. Paul, Minnesota. I was there to start a new program for public radio called *Good Evening*. Garrison Keillor had left us the theater and the Saturday time slot and an audience accustomed to some pretty good music over the years of *A Prairie Home Companion;* this was the piano on which Butch Thompson played his Jelly Roll Morton tunes. It was a Steinway, a nine-foot concert grand, Model D, with a German action (people would say knowingly). It was a piano that *satisfied* players. Billy Taylor would come out from New York to play jazz on our program, walk in the stage entrance from the alley, say hello, take off his coat, wander over to center stage —when you travel playing piano, this is a moment of dread—and sit down and play a few chords and not be able to hold back a real grin. Marian McPartland also had a dandy time, playing "Emily" and "I'm Old Fashioned." (We went out for dinner afterward. The restaurant had a high-tech player piano, a Yamaha. Marian listened for a moment, looking at the keys moving up and down, watching in effect the playing of a ghost, and she said, "Why, that's Teddy." And indeed it was Teddy Wilson's music programmed into the piano's computer.)

Liz Story brought her thoughtful New Age jazz arrangements. Kate McGarrigle played the sad chords of "Talk to Me of Mendocino," while she sang with her sister, Anna. And Harry Connick, Jr., then twenty-one and not at all well known, *startled* the audience. Big, bangy New Orleans chords and walking bass lines and audacious tempo changes. He'd tell you about Professor Longhair and Dr. John and James Booker, the music that came to his hands growing up.

When Harry Connick led our band through some rocking blues to close the show that night—a big finish with everybody clapping—I stood right beside him, at his left. I wanted to *feel* that music. I never saw anybody have that much fun at the piano.

During the week, at quiet moments when the theater was dark, I'd approach the Steinway. I'd sit down and sound a single note, softly, and hear it floating above nine hundred empty seats. I knew a fragment of one chord, and I could remember a few notes in a bass pattern, but mostly I'd just touch keys at random: sweet, stirring, dissonant, bluesy. The piano was so good it sounded as if I could play it.

Six years went by. Neenah and I were in New York one Saturday, to visit some friends. "Let's go to Steinway Hall," I said. "I've always wanted to see all those pianos there together." Many years ago I'd interviewed the pianist Gary Graffman and we talked in the Steinway basement, the "selection room" where the concert pianos are kept, and I did a story once about a piano moving company in Manhattan—their crews were in and out of Steinway every day—but I'd missed seeing the showrooms upstairs.

"Let's go," Neenah said, and we went up to West Fifty-seventh Street and entered Erica vanderLinde Feidner's world. She happily and patiently sells Steinway pianos and spent an hour showing us Model Ss and Ms and Ls and Bs and Ds. It's said—not by Steinway people, you understand—that S means "small" and M stands for "medium," L for "large," B for "big," and D for "damn big." The D is the concert grand—the model we had at the World Theater. Erica tells you the price for the D, and all you can do is laugh: $62,300. You spend time at the smaller models, a touch here and there to the gleam of mahogany or a shining ebony finish; you press down a few keys, hesitantly (off in other rooms you can hear *great* players trying to make *their* choices).

"Do you play?" Erica asks.

"Oh, no, not at all."

She does, helpfully. Gentle, falling chords from a prelude by Chopin (I asked). Erica comes from a family of seven pianists and teachers. She started at age three, was studying at Juilliard at nine, and later bought her own Steinway grand with prize money from the Miss America Pageant. She was Miss Vermont and won the talent competition in Atlantic City.

Well, perhaps an upright. Here's the Model K, it's fifty-two inches tall, quite nice. And the Professional 1098. Forty-six inches. We're assured these are *very* good pianos, and probably an upright would be all we have money for, or space. Last year we could have had a great deal on a small Weber grand. Our neighbors were replacing it with a family-heirloom Steinway. But we realized we'd have to put the piano in our living room. Which would then be a piano room.

So the upright? We could go home and measure? Sure, Erica said. Here's the brochure, pictures of all the models, a price list. Here's my card. She smiled and said good-bye to us as if she expected a call on Monday, and we went to a restaurant around the corner for a plate of pasta and I asked for a glass of wine, feeling that we'd escaped. "Wasn't she nice," Neenah said.

On the train ride back to Washington I thought some about the piano, and back to a story that stays with me from Vance Bourjaily's novel *The Man Who Knew Kennedy*. The setting is the sixties, after John Kennedy's assassination, with flashbacks to the time when JFK and the young men of the novel were still in college, but soon to go to war. Barney James, the book's narrator, has been teaching a classmate to play "Skylark" on the piano, teaching it by rote, finger by finger, note by note. Tommy Angus started with "Sky-" and learned "-lark" and went on from there. He had someone he wanted to play it for. He imagined "the moment when the lovely blonde girl would be at the spring house party with him and would mention that she liked the song. And Tommy, dressed for the formal dance perhaps, would smile, and set down his glass of Scotch, sit, pretend some brief confusion, and then smoothly play it through for her. . . ." It didn't work out with the girl, and the party turned out to be somber, but Tommy Angus did play. "Play it, Tommy. Play 'Skylark.' " His friend, his teacher, recalled the moment decades later:

We have our arms around girls, most of us, and he is playing for us. But of course he is playing for himself too, and for the girl who isn't there. He changes the bright, melodious little song, with its occasional minor passages, into something I never taught him, slow and melancholy and graceful, with impeccable rhythm. It is going to haunt me, played like that, all through the war at odd moments. I will hear it when I'm flying alone sometimes, maybe when I land and cut the motor, or late at night after a mission when I'm last man at the bar at the Officer's Club and the record player has stopped.

When you can't play the piano, you think, yes, maybe you could learn to play one fairly complicated song pretty well. I keep hearing a slow blues, played at a thinking speed, like an improvisation. The tune would come to a slow ending with hushed chords, and I'd close the piano lid and walk out into a clear, cold night (this used to involve a cigarette, but I quit nine years ago and don't even smoke in fantasies anymore).

Then there was Jane Campion's *The Piano*. We'd just seen the movie and still talked about it. Holly Hunter plays Ada, a Scottish woman who does not speak, although as the film begins, we do hear her voice: "The strange thing is I don't think myself silent, that is, because of my piano. I shall miss it on the journey." Ada travels with her daughter and her piano out to New Zealand to begin an arranged marriage. Their belongings are carried ashore and then up into the craggy green hills. But the piano is abandoned, left to stand by itself at the edge of the incoming water. We begin to feel Ada's obsession with the instrument and with music. She carves a keyboard in the wood of a table and plays silently. The piano is retrieved; a tuner is summoned, a blind man. "A fine instrument," he says. And he sniffs the air near the keys. "Scent? And salt, of course." But Ada's new husband has made a deal with one of his friends: Her piano has been traded for some land. The friend has Ada in mind more than the piano, and she agrees to earn the piano back with an escalation of sexual favors, beginning with the slightest lifting of her skirts as she plays. Holly Hunter is actually playing the piano in her scenes for this movie; she had years of lessons, growing up. It's music that sounds vaguely classical with touches of Scotland, music that changes with Ada's moods.

The Piano is a story of suppressed desire, jealousy, violence. You leave the theater saying, "What was that really about?" And "How could her piano be that important?" (A discussion group was held in Washington, D.C., on these questions, led by the Forum for the Psychoanalytic Study of Film: "Topics include the mutism of Ada, voyeurism, mutilation and the meaning of Ada's piano.")

And I have been thinking about the death in December of Lewis Thomas, a writer whose work I'd long admired. The *New York Times* called Dr. Thomas "the poet-philosopher of medicine." He'd been the dean of the Yale School of Medicine, he won a National Book Award for his essays on science and nature, but the *Times* obituary mentioned two regrets he'd expressed while in his mid-seventies: He had wanted to speak "impeccable" French, and he said, "I wish I could play the piano."

I knew I had no talent for language, so Dr. Thomas's yearning for French didn't speak to me. But his thoughts about the piano stayed close for days after I read of his death. He *should* have learned piano. He had been on a long search for music's meaning, and power. He believed that music is "the effort we make to explain to ourselves how our brains work." And he was convinced that music is at nature's center. In his book *The Lives of a Cell* Dr. Thomas imagined an orchestra of earthworm instrumentalists, and crickets and the voices of whales. "If we had better hearing," he wrote, "and could discern the descants of sea birds, the rhythmic timpani of schools of mollusks, or even the distant harmonics of midges hanging over meadows in the sun, the combined sound might lift us off our feet."

I called New York a couple of times, to talk with

Erica vanderLinde Feidner about the various Model Ks she had in stock, pianos with different finishes and tone personalities. I realized I was beginning to think about *which* piano rather than *if* a piano. On Christmas Eve, a Friday, I had the day off and took a morning shuttle flight up to La Guardia and a cab to Fifty-seventh Street.

I was close to deciding on the bigger upright, the Model K, at $15,700. Erica had two of them waiting for me, side by side (with blue "selected" tags). One piano had a softer tone; the other had a lighter key action. Erica left me alone and closed the door. I played a few notes on both Model Ks, but it wasn't fun; I was too anxious. I walked over to a grand and tried the touch (quite different, Erica explained, from that of an upright). It was silky and quick. *Oh, that's what I want*, I thought, but it cost thousands more. Then I noticed one of the smaller uprights, the Model 1098. Played fine, wasn't *intimidating*. Has the word *Professional* in the name. It has a sleek look. Get it in black, it's $500 less than mahogany. But somehow I just couldn't say, sure, that's the one I'll take.

Back home in Washington I talked some with Neenah. I was thinking that paying that kind of money for a piano was reckless. And could I actually learn to play it? She seemed relieved that I hadn't made a decision. A few years ago a friend of ours, a jazz recording engineer, bought a Steinway Model B for $25,000 and only then faced the problem of telling his wife and figuring out how they might pay for it. (I've often mentioned this to Neenah. The last time she said, "What's the point of that story?") And we have made a commitment to help a young Sarajevo woman whom Neenah had met there last fall. Šejla Bezdrob worked as an interpreter for the visiting journalists; there was a chance she could get press credentials and then leave Bosnia. She wanted to come to Washington and go to college. She was eighteen years old and trusted Neenah. No one could say if this idea would work or what it might cost.

But one morning three weeks later I called Steinway Hall in New York and spent $11,375. We were in the kitchen of a bed-and-breakfast outside Taos, New Mexico, on vacation. Neenah was across the room, putting jelly on toast. I hung up the phone. She said, "You just did it?" But I could tell she was pleased that we'd have a piano in the house and that now I'd quit being so worried about deciding. I bought the Model 1098 (the price includes the piano bench, the first tuning, and $675 shipping cost). In the end it was just as if I had called Steinway one sky blue day and said, "Send me down the cheapest thing you've got."

The moment came when I was sitting at the table drinking coffee and looking out the kitchen window at Tres Orejas, a spiky mountain sitting all by itself out to the west, twenty miles away. We'd had a long night's sleep after some strenuous hiking. Three days earlier, as we were leaving Washington for New Mexico, we'd heard the first reports of a massive earthquake in Los

Angeles. I suppose I could have delayed my vacation; I work for a daily news program, *All Things Considered*, on National Public Radio. I even could have flown straight on to California to help cover the story. We needed the time off, though. I'd had a difficult year, which included a reporting trip to Serbia, just two months after I broke my collarbone and cracked three ribs in a bicycle accident. Neenah—a freelance journalist —had finished her exhausting and dangerous assignment in Sarajevo. Christmas was over, relatives had been visited, snowstorms were coming to the East Coast, and we longed for the high desert sun and hot spices of northern New Mexico. The mountains are gray and green and fragrant with sagebrush and piñon and you can walk for hours and anything seems possible. Play the piano? Sure.

FEBRUARY

An extrafine Taos morning and a ten-thousand-dollar phone call

"THERE ARE THREE GUYS IN A TRUCK COMING DOWN INTER-state 95 with your piano!"

It was a pretty loud voice inside my mind. Surely I'd made an awful, expensive mistake. And when do I have time for this? I figure I've only got an extra twenty minutes a day in which I can pay any attention at all to anything not connected with work or with keeping the house from falling down. Once Neenah and I went through an entire year refusing to realize that our car's windshield wipers were broken and wouldn't turn on.

My spare twenty minutes come right after dinner, twenty minutes before I fall asleep in a chair trying to read. Usually I'll struggle with it for a while; then I'll take a hot bath and get in bed, where suddenly I'm awake again. Seven or so books wait on the table by the bed. One will be by an author I'm soon to interview, the others are interesting-looking books that probably I *should* read, and another will be something that's already past its story-potential time, to read just for pleasure, a few pages a night.

Then the reading at last becomes dreaming, and sometimes as I reach over to turn out the light, I'm quite happy because I've had a couple of truly insightful thoughts, about my life or NPR or the world. Profound realizations that of course I can't recall in the morning —just like marijuana insights in the old days. More often, though, I'm thinking about stories coming up tomorrow or even a question I failed to ask today.

I'm up about 6:30 A.M. to feed Will, the dog, and listen to the radio and turn on the television and go out front to pick up the *Washington Post* and the *New York Times*. I'll have about an hour with coffee and the papers; then Neenah's up, and Bonny, the younger dog, and it's a race for the bathroom and breakfast and forgetting things and a fast walk to the Metro station and a ride to work reading *USA Today*. (I don't know how people with children get a single day accomplished.) On the bad mornings I'm eating toast with peanut butter as I leave the house. The day ends about twelve hours later; quite often it's nine o'clock before we sit down to dinner.

Occasionally you'll see in the Washington paper a

story about some administration wizard, talented, dedicated, finally at the center of power. The *Post* "Style" section profile will have a paragraph about the official's daily schedule, and you'll read this in the morning when you've overslept and you're sitting there scratching yourself. For example, of Strobe Talbott, President Clinton's deputy secretary of state, the *Post* says: "This is Strobe Talbott's life: Up at 5 A.M. to read or write or play classical guitar. Jog at 6:15 A.M., Garrison Keillor on the headphones. Workout at 6:45 A.M. Breakfast and an intelligence brief at the State Department by 7:30 A.M." Maybe if I can get this piano thing going and manage to wake up earlier, I could get together with Strobe for a little duet action around 5:30.

The morning the three guys came with the piano I'd stayed home from work. "It's important," I'd told my producer. "I'd like to be there." The truck backed up the driveway at ten o'clock. Fox Piano Movers, out of Philadelphia. Two big guys and a driver named Charlie, who came inside the house to check for tricky doorways. We'd been wondering how they'd get the piano through the hallway and around the corner into our office. "No problem," Charlie said.

The men open the back door of the truck, and there's my upright Steinway piano, covered with a brown quilted blanket. They unstrap it and roll it down a ramp and into the house, tilt it up on its side on a dolly, and ease it into the office. A piano—moved. Charlie's happy. I sign the papers; they use the bathroom, make a phone call, and then take off. The unloading took less than thirty minutes. Neenah told me later that she was thinking it would be nice if babies could arrive the same way.

I sit alone with a Professional Model 1098. It's black, "Ebonized," a shiny finish but not glossy; the wood inside has a warm light. The three brass pedals are covered by green felt booties, tied with red string. The piano needs to warm up after the truck ride, but I sit and play the first notes, gently, to see what the tone's like, and several keys together with my left hand, just guessing at chords. Sounds pretty good. This might be okay.

But now what? A few years ago Neenah bought a good violin, paid a thousand dollars. She's got a great ear and loves music; she played bassoon in her high school concert band. Our neighbor, a serious amateur chamber player, started giving her lessons. But it was hard work, beginning, and she didn't have enough time, and now the violin waits in the closet, where she doesn't have to be confronted with it. A neglected piano surely would be bothersome every time you walked in the room.

The music comes so much easier, though, on the piano. A violin defies you to produce a lovely sound, the trumpet can tear you up trying to play it, but the piano works right away—a child can do it. And sometimes a child can *really* do it. There's always a familiar sentence or two in the autobiographies of pianists:

"I was born with music inside me. Like my blood.

And from the moment I learned that there were keys to be mashed, I started mashing 'em, trying to make sounds out of feelings."—Ray Charles.

"From the beginning I could play a melody I'd heard only once, and make up pieces on the piano by just doodling."—Judy Collins.

"I learned [at age three] to call the keys by their names, and with my back to the piano I would call the notes of any chord, even the most dissonant one."—Arthur Rubinstein.

And imagine this: "At the Presleys' he was always fooling around on the piano, picking out a tune that they might have heard on the radio—he could play anything after hearing it once or twice, nothing fancy, simply sticking to the melody. Sometimes he would sit at the piano and just sing hymns." That's a description of a very young Elvis Presley, from Peter Guralnick's *Last Train to Memphis*. There's a picture of Elvis on the cover of the book. He's alone in a room, sitting at an old upright. And he can be *heard* playing piano, in the Sun recording studio, on the 1955 song "Trying to Get to You." This could be the same piano that Jerry Lee Lewis started tearing up two years later; he'd come to Memphis to work as a session player for Sun Records. Presley and Lewis both had the dynamic originality and spirit that Sun's owner, Sam Phillips, liked so much. Phillips had worked as a radio announcer and engineer for big band broadcasts from a Memphis hotel, but the music was "too slick" for him, the songs always the same. He's quoted in the liner notes for a Sun Records collection: "What I was aiming to do . . . was to get to a certain area, a certain province, of human emotion. I wanted to see if what I had thought all my life—that there was something very profound in the life of people with less means when it came to money, less means when it came to social acceptance—was right or wrong." When Elvis started singing the old blues song "That's All Right (Mama)" one day in the studio, Phillips recognized the sound he was waiting for: "This is where the soul of man never dies." And of Jerry Lee's music, he said, "He never played a damn song back-to-back the same way. He didn't want to do it, he couldn't do it."

The rest of us wind up with the music books. For Christmas Neenah gave me *Teaching Little Fingers to Play: A Book for the Earliest Beginner.* It's a John Thompson book, from the Willis Music Company in Florence, Kentucky, and I figure if I ever misplace it someday, I can just go knocking on neighbors' doors and find a copy inside the first piano bench. She also gift wrapped her own John Thompson book from thirty-five years ago: *For Girls Who Play.* "Neenah Ann Ellis" is written in large script at the bottom of the orange cover, and her teacher's penciled notes indicate the tempo and the fingering for songs like "The Swing" and "The Lame Dog" and "Gathering Wild Flowers" ("Over the hills and the fields we go/Big girls and little girls all in a row/Harder than bees we'll work/Not a hand here shall shirk/Till all our arms are with blooms aglow").

Also under the Christmas tree: "Clair de Lune," by Debussy, a simplified arrangement. And a "Big Note Piano Series" edition of "Linus and Lucy," one of the Peanuts' songs by Vince Guaraldi. The "Linus and Lucy" tempo is given as "moderately bright," and it occurs to me that I hadn't been thinking about playing anything any faster than "slow."

We decide to go see André Watts at the Kennedy Center. Big time, dress up, drive downtown Saturday night. This is the twentieth time Mr. Watts has performed at the Concert Hall. It's the first time I've been to a classical piano recital, and I suppose it's good to start with a superstar. It's a sold-out event, twenty-seven hundred people. I notice a lot of single men in the audience.

I love the time just before a performance begins. There's a soft crackle of expectation that seems to run through the hall. Light, nervous laughter. The piano— stating the challenge of the evening ahead—rests on the bare wooden floor at the precise center of the stage.

If you want to see André Watts actually playing, if you want to watch his hands, you should try to get seats in the left side of the Concert Hall. "Keyboard view" is the term. I've been curious about how it was decided that the pianist always sits with his or her right side to the audience, and the answer turns out to be simple:

The piano's lid is hinged on the left side; when it's opened the sound can flow out.

And history has saved the name of the first pianist to use this placement onstage. In his book *The Great Pianists* Harold Schonberg explains that once pianists played only at private salons. When public concerts became popular, someone had to decide where the pianist would sit. In the late 1700s, Schonberg writes, Jan Ladislav Dussek "solved the problem once and for all time. He was the first to sit with his right side to the audience. Dussek was able to exhibit his noble profile and the bow of the piano; and the raised lid of the instrument could act as a sounding board, throwing tone directly into the audience. . . . By the age of twenty he was racing all over Europe, exhibiting his profile to ecstatic audiences."

Clara Schumann became the first pianist to play recitals from memory. She was criticized for this. Many people thought it was insulting to the composer to perform without the score. And Franz Liszt, in 1839, was the first to play a public recital all alone, without orchestra or singers. He wrote later that he was saying to the audience, "*le concert, c'est moi.*"

Our Mr. Watts is resplendent in white tie and tails as he walks out, smiling. He sits, adjusts the bench, and begins, my *Stagebill* tells me, Mozart's Rondo in D Major, K. 485. He plays on through Beethoven and Schubert, and after the intermission, Janáček, Berio, Liszt, and Chopin. We are sitting high up near the back row of the second balcony, but even from here the piano sounds splendid, and my mind drifts away with the music. On Monday at work a colleague who had brought her young son to the concert said, "We were sitting about four rows behind you; I saw you sleeping."

"I really enjoyed it," I said.

The concert did have a businesslike ending, though. Mr. Watts didn't play an encore. He came back out, responding to the applause, and spoke to the audience: "Those of you who have seen me play know that I enjoy playing encores, but I'm having a bit of unimportant back pain and I need to call it a night."

The next day the review in the *Washington Post* spoke of André Watts's "fabulous . . . unromantic" Beethoven, said his Schubert "glistened," and judged his playing of Liszt's *Les Jeux d'Eaux à la Villa d'Este* to be "clear, bright, penetrating."

It would certainly have been different to have heard Franz Liszt play the work. Harold Schonberg writes: "When Liszt played the piano, ladies flung their jewels on the stage instead of bouquets. They shrieked in ecstasy and sometimes fainted." And consider the response of Moritz Gottlieb Saphir, a male music critic, writing a century and a half ago:*

Liszt . . . is an amiable fiend who treats his mistress —the piano—now tenderly, now tyrannically, de-

---

* From *Men, Women, and Pianos: A Social History* by Arthur Loesser.

vours her with kisses, lacerates her with lustful bites, embraces her, caresses her, sulks with her, scolds her, rebukes her, grabs her by the hair, clasps her then all the more delicately, more affectionately, more passionately, more flamingly, more meltingly; exults with her to the heavens, soars with her through all the skies and finally settles down with her in a vale of flowers covered by a canopy of stars. . . . After the concerts Liszt stands there like a victor on the battlefield, like a hero at a tournament. Daunted pianos lie around him; torn strings wave like flags of truce; frightened instruments flee into distant corners; the listeners look at each other as after a cataclysm of nature that has just passed by . . . and he stands there leaning melancholically on his chair, smiling strangely. . . . Thus is Franz Liszt.

MARCH

Getting past middle C with a computer looking over my shoulder

THERE'S BEEN A SECRET, HIDING IN MY HEART ABOUT THIS piano-learning endeavor. Perhaps I do have talent and no one knows. Does the word *child* necessarily have to be in front of *prodigy*? Let's say the piano arrives. The shipping blanket is removed. The instrument sits in the darkened room, the chilled steel and copper strings warming. Late in the night the owner comes to the bench, quietly eases back the keyboard cover. With a finger of his right hand he sounds an A, the downward movement coming not from the hand as much as from the entire body. The note opens from silence and blossoms. A bass note is struck, with force, a G. And another, a B. The low tones are marching into the night.

There's a rippling of treble. Then a chord in the left hand, an answering chord from the right. A diminished seventh in the bass. The melody begins in response—a welcome for the piano! The owner plays a wandering thought . . . echoes of fifties rock and Ahmad Jamal records and George Shearing and Floyd Cramer. Then the tune resolves into C-sharp minor. A pause. And the notes begin, Adagio sostenuto. The music is Beethoven's Piano Sonata in C-sharp Minor, op. 27, no. 2 (quasi una fantasia), but the owner only knows it has something to do with moonlight. Three notes repeat in the right hand, low, vibrant chords in the left. . . . He plays on, and a soft light comes through the window. In another room the dogs sigh, comfortably, on their cushion in front of the fireplace. In the kitchen the owner's wife, stirring honey into her chamomile tea at bedtime, listens and smiles. She is not surprised.

Or maybe it could work this way: In the movie *Groundhog Day* Bill Murray plays an arrogant—"people are morons"—Pittsburgh Action 9-TV weatherman who, while covering Groundhog Day in Punxsutawney, finds himself stuck in time. Precisely the same things happen every day, although he *can* affect events by changing *his* behavior. And he does, trying to become a nicer person to win the love of his producer, Rita (Andie MacDowell). She's mentioned her ideal man would be able to play an instrument, and we see Phil Conners (Murray) make his decision. He's sitting in a restaurant one morning, having coffee, reading the paper. We hear Mozart's Sonata in C, K. 545, from a tape player on a shelf. Phil looks up, pleased. Then a scene at the front door of a house: He rings the bell; a woman comes and says, "Yes?" "I'd like a piano lesson, please." "Oh, okay. I'm with a student now, but if you'd want to come back tomorrow—" "Well, I kind of want to get it started. I can give you a thousand dollars," Phil says, pulling money from his coat pocket. She smiles. "Come on in." An unhappy teenage girl is pushed out the front door, clutching her sheet music. From the house we hear a C major scale, starting with a missed note. Underneath all this the Mozart sonata has continued to play and now comes to a tidy ending. It's happened very quickly; from inspiration to first lesson: one minute five seconds. And then, in another instant, Phil Conners *is* a piano player, wearing shades and playing blues-rock behind the keyboard with a rock band at the Groundhog Dance. When Rita walks in, he grins and shifts to a Rachmaninoff rhapsody.

Actually I did have some lessons when I was about ten years old. "Let's try it," my mother said. A rented piano fit nicely into the front room, I was supposed to practice after school, but there was always more fun outside, and I was never ready on Saturday mornings when I walked the three blocks to my teacher's house. There were two pianos, side by side, in her gloomy front room. She always seemed unhappy with my progress. My only

25

real pleasure anyway was in playing the boogie-woogie patterns, and she knew that wasn't going anywhere.

Many years ago an accomplished pianist and veteran teacher decided you could tell which youngsters were going to be able to play by just looking at them. Helen Hopekirk wrote: "You will find that all musicians have noses that are broad at the base. Always look at a new pupil's nose, and never expect anything of a pupil who has a thin, pinched nose. If the pupil has a nose that is broad at the base, you can feel quite happy." In recounting this story in *The Great Pianists*, Harold Schonberg adds: "Hopekirk had a nose that was *very* broad at the base."

And I've been told to look for an extra-long little finger. That pianists will often have a little finger that extends well past the knuckle of the finger next to it. This is interesting but probably not important; Josef Hofmann, one of the great pianists, had rather small hands. Steinway even made special instruments for Hofmann, with the keys scaled down just a bit.

My own hands seem big enough (even if the little-finger tips fall short of ideal), my nose looks to be unremarkable, and still, after forty years, I remain skeptical of piano teachers.

"Have you found someone yet?" friends ask. "You *will* work with a teacher?"

"Sure," I say, "there's probably someone right here in the neighborhood."

And there is. I see her small ad every month in the *Town Journal*: PIANO LESSONS, ALL AGES AND LEVELS. CONCERT PIANIST. M.A. IN MUSIC. CALL BARBARA KOBER. But I just don't feel up to calling a teacher. I can't picture myself going to someone's house and having to start at middle C, and leaving with the "Ode to Joy" assignment. And I know that some weeks I'd have to skip most of the practicing and the lesson would be wasted, or I'd be out of town on the day of the lesson.

I've been reading ads for the Miracle Piano Teaching System, $259.95. "THE FIRST PIANO THAT TEACHES YOU HOW TO PLAY IT." The copy promises, "By the end of the first lesson, you won't just be playing, you'll be playing along with the Miracle Orchestra!" So instead of calling up a teacher, I use the MacWorld computer catalog 800 number.

My musical future arrives by way of Airborne Express. It was waiting on the doorstep in a long, narrow, brightly colored box, a picture of a keyboard floating in the blue sky amid the fluffy clouds of music heaven—"A professional instrument that grows with you!" Inside there's a keyboard and cables and floppy disks and a manual. The first challenge is to get the Miracle into my computer. This can be a tense operation. The room's a mess and there's not enough light and I'm tired, but I tear open the box and spill out the manual and the floppy disks and the foam-packed keyboard, read the "Quick Installation Card," and go for it. I plug in the keyboard's power adapter, and make the connection to the computer's modem jack. Hit the toggle switch on the back of the keyboard, green lights come on.

"Works with Macintosh," the box says, reassuringly; we have a IIcx. I start loading in the floppy disks. Five of them. The Mac makes clickety-grunts and displays the input progress on the screen, a zippy bar graph. "Installation was successful! You are now ready to use the Miracle Piano Teaching System." But then I double-click the Miracle icon and see on the screen: "Sorry, you cannot operate the Miracle at 256-colors. Use black and white configuration." This has something to do with the Mac's memory and our antique operating system. I change the monitor setting to B&W, then reload the disks. About halfway through the procedure a bong sounds and the screen says, "Sorry, a system error has occurred. Please restart." (At this warning the Mac depicts a small, round bomb with a lit fuse. It's a diabolical graphic that strikes terror.)

Time to go into the kitchen for a bowl of cornflakes, trying to calm down. The computer did restart okay, but probably everything should rest for the night. I put on a new Dr. John CD—and play a song with one of my all-time favorite titles: "Thank You (Falletin Me Be Mice Elf Again)," and the crunchy New Orleans piano playing bounces me right up out of the computer worries. Dr. John has an autobiography out, and I'll be talking with him in a couple of weeks.

I remember a rock and roll piano story from an interview some years ago. Geoffrey Stokes of the *Village Voice* had written a book about Commander Cody and His Lost Planet Airmen band, as they struggled to make an album. This was a great live stage band, but it was tough to get the excitement cranked up and on tape in the studio. Stokes gave me the perfect example, and we were able to demonstrate it by playing the finished song on the radio; the Airmen's version of "House of Blue Lights," a boogie-woogie piano classic. Commander Cody, whose actual name is George Frayne, had recorded twelve versions, but he was always radically off tempo with the rest of the band. When Frayne took the weekend off, the producer brought in a legendary Los Angeles studio player—Roger Kellaway—to do the track. Kellaway at that time could be heard playing piano on about half of the rock and roll records made on the West Coast. He came into the Sausalito Record Plant, asked for some blank music paper, asked for the tape of "House of Blue Lights" to be played, twice, as he wrote down the notes. An awed musician, watching, said, "He's already amazing. But he can't play it. It's *very* hard."

Kellaway warmed up at the piano, then cautioned, "I don't know if I can play this. It's not the way I play boogie-woogie, but even if it was, it's an impossible key." (The song should have been in C but now was in B-flat, to make it easier for the guy trying to play the trombone.)

Everyone got ready for a take, and Kellaway tried but

couldn't keep his right hand together with his left hand. So he recorded the left hand only with the band, then added the right hand on another track. Everyone's happy except the Commander, who starts yelling when he comes back to California and finds out. "You guys didn't give me a chance. You didn't treat me like a serious musician." Then he sits down at the piano and plays the whole thing perfectly. A compromise: George Frayne will play the top notes instead of Kellaway, resulting, as Geoffrey Stokes put it, "in a record with a piano part recorded by two different people: the left hand by a man who was in Los Angeles when the right hand was recorded by a man who'd been in Philadelphia when the left hand was recorded."

"It's extraordinary how many works there are for left hand alone."—Leon Fleisher.

You can listen to one of the new recordings by Leon Fleisher—the Ravel concerto, for example—and not notice he is playing with one hand. Fleisher made his Carnegie Hall debut at sixteen and went on to become one of this country's great concert pianists. His Beethoven and Brahms recordings with George Szell and the Cleveland Orchestra are still benchmarks. When he was in his mid-thirties, Fleisher lost control of the fingers of his right hand. It was a repetitive stress syndrome injury. He turned to conducting and teaching and didn't play the piano in public for twenty years.

Now Leon Fleisher is again on the concert stage, playing Ravel's Piano Concerto for the Left Hand, plus works by Benjamin Britten and many other composers. Some of the best music was commissioned by a pianist named Paul Wittgenstein, who lost his right arm in the First World War. Mr. Fleisher believes he harmed his right hand as a young player, practicing too hard, trying to fill the concert halls with sound. We talked about this during an interview on *All Things Considered,* just before one of his New York City performances.

LEON FLEISHER: Piano playing has been, to such a large extent over the years, a kind of anecdotal activity passed on from generation to generation, and there are many people who've been able to play incorrectly from a biomedical point of view and not really suffer for it, and they are very lucky. But there are also a large number of people who are not as lucky and who really have to understand what kind of movements are involved with pressing the key down and supporting the weight as well as supporting the energy and the intensity of the purpose and the feeling.

NDA: Well, what specifically are the movements that are endangering to a pianist?

MR. FLEISHER: Oh, one of the things that is passed on is the idea that one uses one's fingers like little hammers. Even if you—if you just rest your hand in front of you on a table and curve the fingers so that the fingers are resting on their fingertips, you have, you know, four little round digits there, and then you attempt to lift them, one after another—you'll see what an awkward and difficult movement that is. If you do that with great force, you know, seven days a week, fifty-two weeks a year, and thirty years more or less nonstop, your hand is very possibly after a while going to say, "No more, no more, stop abusing me." So, I would suggest that a much more natural position is to use the digit from that row of knuckles that join it with the hand; they're called the metacarpals—just use that as a single lever, gently curved maybe, but playing almost very close to the pad of the finger rather than on the tip.

NDA: Anything else?

MR. FLEISHER: That's about it [*laughs*].

NDA: You have said about the Ravel left-hand work—composition—that he said: "One should not notice anything amiss if one should close one's eyes." In other words, that you would be hearing—

MR. FLEISHER:—a normal performance, yes. With the left hand. That was his stated intention.

NDA: Do you think that Ravel accomplished what he was looking for?

MR. FLEISHER: Oh, without question. It happens to be such a wonderful case of serendipity that not only did he achieve what he was going for, but the Ravel concerto, in my opinion at least, is one of the great masterpieces of the musical repertoire—one hand, two hands, seven hands, you know, you name it. It's just one of the great, great works that exists in music.

NDA: Are there any tricks involved in this when we're

hearing it? For example, is there a special pedal technique?

MR. FLEISHER: Not necessarily. I think really the only special thing is that you have to kind of switch your center of gravity. Playing left-hand work, I have to move a little bit higher to the upper register, balance myself differently. Rather than sitting squarely where I sit, I kind of lean on my right buttock a lot more and very often even extend my left leg when I'm leaning very much up towards the top of the keyboard to kind of balance that out. Sometimes it's quite awkward. You know, I've often found myself hanging on to the piano with my right hand—which is, well, I don't feel it's cheating. It's certainly something poor Mr. Wittgenstein wasn't able to do.

NDA: But it's better than falling off the stool.

MR. FLEISHER: It certainly is, I assure you.

NDA: It sounds like quite a workout.

MR. FLEISHER: It can be, it can be.

NDA: When you are reminded of the *New York Times* statement many years ago describing you as the finest American pianist of his or probably any time, it was, what, a full twenty years before you performed again, correct?

MR. FLEISHER: Yeah.

NDA: Was there a time of sadness for you?

MR. FLEISHER: Oh, yes. Absolutely. A time of deep, deep funk. Absolutely. Oh, yes, all kinds of thoughts, including self-destruction and including growing a ponytail and including taking to a Vespa and roaring around the streets of Baltimore, helmetless. Sure.

NDA: But you knew all this time that the left-handed repertoire was out there?

MR. FLEISHER: Yes, but in a sense to accept that and to delve into it meant accepting the condition, and that took me a long while before I was ready for that.

NDA: You're saying that you didn't think that playing left-handed was somehow lesser musicianship than playing—

MR. FLEISHER: No, no, not at all. Actually, I didn't really have much of a clue how much there is for left hand, certainly not at that point. The only piece I was aware of was the Ravel concerto and possibly the Prokofiev Fourth. But no, I discovered there are lots of others, and I am particularly proud—there are several pieces that have been written for me, so in my little, humble way, if you will, I'm somehow responsible for expanding the repertoire for those who will come after me, and that's really satisfying. That's very nice.

After our interview I told Mr. Fleisher that I had bought a piano and hoped to learn to play. "That's great," he said. "How wonderful." I was a bit embarrassed; telling Leon Fleisher about my ambition for piano lessons is like telling Julia Child about plans to make toast in the morning. I wonder what it's like for him, these days, when one of his great Cleveland Orchestra recordings comes on the radio. Does he listen?

Does he wonder how good a player he could have become, given another ten or twenty years?

Leon Fleisher once told this story (in a *Los Angeles Times* article) about his friend George Szell, the Cleveland Orchestra's conductor: "We were playing in London, and Szell invited me to his room to sing through the piece—I think it was the *Emperor* Concerto—because he didn't have a piano in his hotel room. We were sitting at a table and I was drumming, playing the table, while he was singing and whistling [the orchestra's part]. At some point he stopped me and said, 'You made a mistake.' And I said, 'But I've never played this table before.'"

My at-home learning project begins with a push of the computer's on button. I click on the icon for the Miracle System, and the program opens, in trusty black and white. At the prompt I type in my name, my nickname (I don't like nicknames, so let's use "nda") and birth date (4-19-42). "Welcome to the Miracle, Noah." To the left of my computer desk I set up a small table for the Miracle "forty-nine key, professional, velocity-sensitive" keyboard. It has two built-in speakers, volume control, and buttons that make the piano sound like several other instruments, including harpsichord and vibraphone.

Every time you turn on the Miracle you have to listen to an opening song—"Simple Gifts," played by piano, organ, then flutes and blaring trumpets. Interesting only at first hearing. Then the computer screen displays the Conservatory. It's like looking down into a building that's had its roof removed. The different areas: Administration, Arcade, Studio, Practice Room, and Performance Hall. Click on a button labeled "Begin Lessons," and there's a drawing of Beethoven—I *am* starting with "Ode to Joy." You hear a short, simple version of the music and then see Beethoven's correct posture at the eighteenth-century keyboard and pictures of the proper hand position: "Curve your fingers like you're holding a ball. Play with the tips of your fingers, play on the side of your thumb."

Then the Miracle keyboard is shown, and I'm told to play all the black keys. Touch a key and the key on the computer screen goes down. "Play all the pairs of black keys"—the screen keys follow your fingers. "Play all the Ds"—the D keys are the white ones between the black pairs. We play the Cs, to the left of the two black keys, then the Es, to the right. Then a Shooting Gallery comes on-screen, with ducks flying slowly from right to left across a treble clef. If a duck is flying on the C line, we're supposed to play a C as it goes past. Same with the D and E ducks. "Quack" is the reward for playing the right key. I manage to get through it, and the computer says, "Nice shooting. That was perfect." I go on to learn F, the white key one step up from E, and G, the next white key. A quick finger-numbering lesson follows. Then I position my right hand with the number 1 thumb over middle C, and play finger 3, play it again, then finger 4, then finger 5. The computer is pleased. "You have just played the first four notes of 'Ode to Joy.'"

Five more notes to learn, starting on G with the little finger, working all the way down to the thumb. Then six others and the entire first phrase is complete. Add the second phrase, same as the first except for the last three notes. "Good going," the computer says. "How does it feel to be playing the piano, Noah?"

Dress rehearsal coming up. And a new concept: *time*. It is almost casually mentioned, as the metronome is introduced: "A series of sounds much like the ticking of a clock." Playing in correct time is sort of like checking your watch during the day so you can stay on schedule. The metronome starts with "four ticks," and then you play. It's not difficult: "That was perfect!"

Now it's concert time. "The Miracle Orchestra is tuned and ready to go, the audience is waiting, and you are the star performer." The screen announces:

"Ode to Joy"
by Ludwig van Beethoven
performed by Noah Adams

I wait to hear the four beats of the metronome, then start. Dah, dah, dah, dah—*trumpets* are playing with me. Dah, dah, dah, dah—and flutes. It's a silly sound and it's too loud and I almost lose my place laughing. Dah, dah, dah, dah, dahhhh, dah dah—piccolos flourish and horns fanfare. On to the finish, I'm missing a couple of notes. We end in a blare of synthesizer sounds. "Nice going, Noah. There's much more to learn, but you can play your first song. You're a piano player!" I'm entitled to print out a certificate to prove that I've completed Lesson 1.

Neenah and I have been talking about what it means to be a piano player. When can one say, "I can play the piano"? She believes that moment comes when emotion can be expressed and heard in one's playing, when human contact can be made. I think it's when you have the ability to work through the sheet music for a song you'd like to play, or especially to understand key signatures and chord progressions and to be able to sit down and improvise. If I can come to the piano late at night and *think* there, drifting through slow blues chords and wandering melodies, or play the old Methodist hymns as they come to mind, then I'd be a piano player. Not a *pianist,* though; Leon Fleisher is a pianist.

Springtime arrives on a Sunday afternoon. I notice the clear, almost pale green light. Neenah's away, working twelve-hour days, weekends as well, helping design and produce the sound track for an upcoming Discovery Channel documentary on D Day, the fiftieth anniversary of the Normandy invasion. I went out early in the morning to buy her some salt bagels (and cream cheese with chives—a spring taste, she said). After breakfast we poked around in the backyard garden, neglected since late summer. The sorrel is coming back strong, and thyme. I don't think I'll bother with peas this spring; they've never worked for me. The ground looks good, though, after several years of compost and bags of sand and manure. In the front yard there's an old tree stump hole which I keep covered with leaves all winter, protecting about fifteen daffodil bulbs. I push aside the leaves and find the muted green-yellow stalks, waiting for light. Low above the trees to the east, a half-moon rises.

All my extra time is being spent at the computer with the Miracle, and some nights it's frustrating. The Miracle keys are slick and feel small and produce electronic tones that squawk and thrum. You don't have to use the keyboard that comes with the system; it works with many of the models that are already on the market, and then you would just buy the Miracle's teaching program. A better sound would help, especially when I'm tired and things start sounding jangly. Also, I have tinnitus—a silvery, ringing sound that's constantly in my ears. (My mother and brother and I share this affliction, although she puts it in perspective: "You could have something *wrong* with you.") And when I spend the entire day enveloped in radio sounds—newsroom chatter, tapes being edited at double speed (you learn to understand the chipmunk voices), music starting and stopping and going backward, a director talking in your headphones—I'd like some aural peace at home. It feels good then to walk up to the real piano and touch an honest bass note and let it roll out into the room.

But it can be fun playing the Miracle, fooling around with a harpsichord effect, trying a tune out on organ. And after many nights working through the necessary but tedious chapters featuring "Mary Had a Little Lamb," "Twinkle, Twinkle, Little Star," and "My Country 'Tis of Thee," learning about whole notes and half notes and what a scale is and the bass clef and playing my first chords, I arrive at "Heart and Soul." It's the bouncy piece children learn right after "Chopsticks." You play it two to a piano bench. I'm learning the bottom part, the accompaniment, with a few new bass notes, and the right hand playing the chords. And the Aliens arrive to help out; a spaceship appears when it's time for Miracle to demonstrate a tricky new note pattern. The craft hovers above a picture of a keyboard. As notes are sounded, numbered windows light up on the spacecraft. The corresponding key lights up below. I play the keys following the order set by the ship. It's exactly the scene from *Close Encounters of the Third Kind*, using music to establish a dialogue between humans and aliens. If you mess up the pattern, you'll be reprimanded: "Your failure to play the correct sequence demonstrates that you have not reached the level of cosmic brotherhood—prepare to be barbequed." If you learn the notes right and can repeat them fast enough, you'll please the Aliens; seven tiny creatures leap into the air. And once this message appeared: "Attention nda the earthling. The Miracle Aliens have chosen you as their ruler. From now on your height will be their standard unit of measurement."

I have a lot of trouble with "Heart and Soul." It's hard for me to play in the proper time. The computer fusses when it's time for evaluation: "You neglected to play many of the notes in these chords." Or "You misplayed the third note (C) in the second measure of the treble clef. It looks like you might have used the wrong finger and played an F instead of the C." But I learn enough to play the song with Neenah. She remembers the melody, one finger at a time.

And she is also part of the great "Bingo" mystery. It's the kid's song about a farmer and his dog: "B-i-n-g-o, Bingo was his name, oh." In Chapter Six "Bingo" helps explain what a key is and how flats are used, and the interval of a fourth. The B-flat is the first black key I've played—it's a big moment—and you can hear that the song wouldn't work without it. I spend a couple of hours with "Bingo," going through the six phrases of the song, the right hand, then the left, then together, then faster, and faster still. My reward is a real out-loud laugh. It comes when I try "Bingo" with the Miracle Jug Band. To the ordinarily corny accompaniment they have added two dogs, barking, as musical punctuation. I'm going along trying to play up to speed when a dog starts barking. Our real dog, Will, who likes to lie on the floor nearby when I'm practicing, jumps up, barking, looking bewildered. I play the song for Neenah. She's delighted and wants to try it herself. The music runs away from her, she's barely hitting any of the notes, it's really a mess, and suddenly we hear the screeching of tires and a dog, yelping in pain. It's mixed into the music in the computer. Neenah played so badly the dog's been hit by a car! Since then I have performed "Bingo" several times, with careless rhythm and lots of wrong notes, but the dogs just bark on cue. I've never again heard the tires screech and the dog yelping. I figure it was a private pleasure in one long day of a computer programmer somewhere.

APRIL

| *The oldest piano in the world plus the sweet inspirations of rock and roll*

APRIL OPENS WARM. YOU CAN SMELL THE EARTH FOR THE first time, and the neighborhood is splashed with the yellow of daffodils and forsythia. I bought arugula and red oak lettuce seedlings at a greenhouse, and the first asparagus should be up soon. On Easter Sunday we turn the clock ahead one hour, go for a swim at the YMCA in the afternoon, have a friend over for roast lamb.

I'm recovering a bit from a frantic day Friday, putting together an April Fools' story for *All Things Considered*. (We just barely made it; the piece was still three minutes too long ten minutes before it was supposed to air.) Last year on April 1 we ran a feature about edible compost, people describing how good their organic compost piles started looking to them, and their decision to eat the compost—mixing it with flour for bread, making compost tea, compost lasagna—instead of using it to fertilize the garden. This year it's "Corporate Tattoos." Big companies like Nike and Pepsi are involved. They offer teenagers a 10 percent discount for life if the kids agree to have brand-name logos tattooed on their earlobes. The tattooing would be done instantly by high-tech lasers. The "Laser Splash" design would include a bar code so the credit could be scanned in right at the cash register. We sent a reporter to talk with youngsters at Washington's Union Station: "If it was cute, I'd wear it, sure." Another said, "If I get a ten percent discount someplace like the Gap where it's expensive anyway." Most of the kids accepted this concept, easily, and I was really surprised at how willing the corporate PR people were to go along; we had statements from Pepsi and Apple, and Keith Peters of Nike said, "You know, you go to a college basketball game these days and you see a Duke Blue Devil painted on the cheerleader's cheeks or you see a Michigan M on a fan's cheeks. So this isn't that far removed from what is already happening." I'd also like to do an April Fools' story about turning various Washington landmarks into private restaurants; they would be open in the evenings after the tourists leave. And I know of a great sound effect for this piece. Some producers I know once made a tape of a grand piano falling, crashing, down all the steps inside the Washington Monument. It sure sounded real.

Two of my radio friends are mentioned in the newspaper as possible replacements for Charles Kuralt on the CBS program *Sunday Morning*. Both are piano players.* Susan Stamberg is a fine sight reader. "Don't waste time memorizing; put the music up there and play it," she tells me. Susan loves show tunes; she's done great interviews with her songwriter heroes: Sammy Cahn, Jule Styne, Betty Comden and Adolph Green. And she's dreamed of playing in an elegant lounge, wearing a red dress, playing a glossy black piano. One night on vacation in Rehoboth Beach, Delaware, at the Back Porch Café, Susan *did* play. She'd noticed the piano at lunch, talked with the manager, returned that evening with some music and her husband. It was, as it turned out, a long *orange* dress with a slit up the side. She played and even sang a bit and laughed with the audience and they *listened* and applauded and Lou sat back, grinning.

And I didn't know that John Hockenberry was a pianist until I read an advance copy of his book: *Moving Violations: War Zones, Wheelchairs, and Declarations of Independence.* John's now with ABC Television. He worked at NPR for ten years, as a newscaster, correspondent, and program host. He was injured in a car accident in 1976 and is a paraplegic; he has full use of his arms and shoulders but not his legs. John writes:

---

*As it turned out, an excellent piano player did get the job— Charles Osgood of CBS.

I moved to the West Coast in the late seventies to get away from family, snow, and the places I had known as a walking person. I lived by myself in a little one-bedroom apartment in Springfield, Oregon, across the McKenzie River from Eugene. I had my camera, an enlarger, my guitars, a Fender Rhodes 77-key electric piano and some books. I spent my days and nights practicing the piano with my headphones on. Loggers and their families lived in the apartments around me and there was lots of screaming from arguing spouses and roomies and their sobbing children.

He was playing Bach and Beethoven, getting ready for an audition at the University of Oregon's School of Music. He lived on food stamps, a small insurance check, worked in an adult rehabilitation center, met Alice, fell in love, got married, and, after two years of practicing, played for three members of the piano faculty. A Bach prelude, some Chopin. He did not, could not, use the pedals, and compensated as best he could by holding some of the notes longer. A professor said about the Chopin, "It's clever what you are doing there with your hands. I suppose you would have to play it that way." But the department chairman said, "There is too much pedaling in modern performance. Pedal turns the clear lines of Mozart and Beethoven into mud." And John was accepted, although he was advised to stay with music written before the 1800s, thereby avoiding the challenge of the pedals. He agreed, while remaining tantalized by the romantic lingering lines of Liszt and Schumann and Brahms. "I dreamed of how I might make the pedals work. Sometimes I would ask Alice to hold down the pedal while I listened to the open strings ring and echo off each other. The harmonics of each string ascended across the sound board like tall crystal ladders in a stately procession of sound, an infinity of tolling bells that vanished when she let go of the pedal. The felt dampers slipped back down on the strings, burying my dream bells in soft wool."

So John set about building a device that would push the sustain pedal down for him. He went to junk shops and rolled along the aisles of industrial specialty stores and talked with inventors and bought a scuba diving tank. His contraption eventually worked. He would hold a rubber bulb between his teeth, bite down at the proper time; compressed air would power a piston that would push the pedal down and hold it there until he unclenched his teeth. The debut was at a recital. John played Erik Satie's *Gymnopédies*, a piece that relies on sustained pedal. "To the audience it was a triumph. They gave me a standing ovation."

It was a triumph, but he understood it would take money and big-time engineering to make the device practical, using precise, computer-driven motors. It was suggested he play the harpsichord, which doesn't have pedals. And he did for a time, even though he was disdainful at first: "The no-pedal option, I imagined, was the cowardly one, as though harpsichords were invented in medieval Europe to give disabled war veterans from the Crusades a musical instrument they could play in their Special Education classes." But John was drifting away from a career in music. "I knew I didn't want it that much," he writes, adding "there might be other things I might want that much someday." Soon he was to volunteer to work in the news department of NPR affiliate KLCC in Eugene. And thus begins the adventure of the rest of his book.

I've since read a master's thesis by a student at California State University, Long Beach, titled "Playing the Piano Without Pedals." Claudio Castagnone, who also lost the use of his legs in a traffic accident, had been playing without pedals for about seven years at the time of his master's recital. Mr. Castagnone writes: "I have performed pieces which ordinarily would not be attempted in public without pedals; nevertheless, I believe I was successful in rendering a meaningful and musical performance." In his thesis he outlines several finger and hand and forearm techniques and positions designed to allow the notes to hold and flow without the pedal to sustain them, allowing phrases to be connected. His musical examples come from Liszt, Chopin, and Ravel. One problem remains unsolved: When you play an A and engage the pedal at the same time, the other As on the piano—because the dampers are lifted off the strings —sound in sympathic vibration. Other overtones are heard as well.

Mr. Castagnone advises: "The pianist should keep in

mind, while examining pieces to determine if they will be playable, without the pedals, that the exact fullness and sonority of the sustaining pedal cannot be duplicated; however, the sounds produced will have clarity and distinction of tone as well as some of the 'wet' effects associated with the sustaining pedal."

My great-grandfather would have been intrigued by this challenge of piano and pedal. Haskell Wellman was an inventor, and he played the violin; I heard him late at night as a child, the music rising up through the house. He was quite old then and stayed to himself, tinkering at his workbench in a dusty, cluttered room, his meals brought to the door. He'd started the telephone company in our town, years earlier, and once owned the first electric automobile dealership. There was a barn out back filled with the parts and tools and benches and harnesses of his work. It's a shame I was too far away from him in age; he had no time for great-grandkids.

The pianoforte itself—today's piano—comes from the mind and the workshop of an Italian craftsman, Bartolomeo Cristofori. He was a harpsichord maker from Padua, brought to Florence to take care of the instruments owned by Prince Ferdinand de' Medici. In 1709 he built a different sort of harpsichord, one that offered a dynamic range: from soft (piano) to loud (forte). With the harpsichord the strings are plucked and all the notes have the same loudness. Cristofori had devised a way to *strike* the strings with a hammer. A magazine article two years later described the *nuova invenzione*, "no less cleverly thought out than executed by Mr. Bartolomeo Cristofali [the magazine had a bit of trouble with the name] in the employ of His Serene Highness the Prince of Tuscany. He has thus far constructed three specimens, of the usual size of ordinary harpsichords, and they have been a complete success."

Arthur Loesser, writing in his book *Men, Women, and Pianos*, offers an opinion as to why the inventor would be an Italian: "For a hundred years before Cristofori, 'expression' had been one of the chief concerns of Italian musicians and their hearers. It was the Italians who, late in the sixteenth century, had created the opera, with its preoccupation with solo singing and the surges and droops natural to it."

The Italians also wanted their instruments to sing, and the seventeenth century was the era of great violins —Stradivari's "golden period." But we do not know Cristofori's thinking on these matters. A quotation would be helpful. Maybe he told a friend, "Gee, these harpsichords sure are boring." You could of course hear organs in the late seventeenth century, but the organ keys could not affect the *volume* of the notes. In Germany the clavichord was popular, somewhat like a harpsichord, but it was cheaper and folksy. It was a rectangular box with strings; the keys would push a blade called a tangent up against the strings. Some volume control *was* possible, but the sound was being dampened as it was being made—the tangent's release was slow—so the clavichord was a quiet instrument, without much tone. There was also in Germany, as the century turned, quite a spectacular dulcimer player. The dulcimer is a stringed instrument that originated in the Middle East and was adopted in Europe in the Middle Ages. It resembles a piano; the player uses mallets to strike the notes. A man named Pantaleon Hebenstreit made his dulcimer sound like an orchestra. He had a huge double instrument built, six feet long and two hundred strings; it had a five-octave range. He could play it whisper-soft and then thundering, with rolling, resonating chords. Pantaleon was a star; he even traveled to France to play for the Sun King, Louis XIV. But it was a singular success: The instrument was impractical to build, and who else could be Pantaleon? So the piano waited offstage in Italy.

Bartolomeo Cristofori went on to build perhaps twenty pianos; you can see a surviving example, an original *gravicembalo col piano e forte* at the Metropolitan Museum of Art in New York. The mechanism he designed—the hammer striking the string and then returning to rest, the vibrations being dampened—is both technically sophisticated and wonderfully crafted and doesn't differ much from today's piano actions.

One night after dinner I open the top of my piano. The uprights have a hinged, flat lid. The front panel above the keyboard will open as well. The piano has not been played much, and never with the top open. I sit down and start the melody of "Heart and Soul," and the notes sing clear and strong. I know I've been avoiding the piano because of the computer lessons. And after an hour of playing on the Miracle keyboard at my desk, the real piano keys feel heavy; my fingers are clumsy finding the notes. The piano, at times, seems cold, and it still smells of new wood and varnish and metal.

I decide to send the Artist's Bench that came with my piano back to Steinway. It has a padded seat, with adjusting knobs on each end. You can move the height up or down by a total of four inches. It's a bit heavy, and it's not real leather. I've talked with Erica in New York, and she'll send down the old reliable black wooden bench, with room under the lid to store music. The pianist Glenn Gould was well known for showing up at recording dates carrying his own special chair. It was a low folding chair his father had adapted; Gould sat fourteen inches off the floor. And the young artist Awadagin Pratt also prefers to be well below the keyboard. He travels with a small wooden table that he sits on.

I've also been concerned about the keyboard on this piano. I notice it seems to be tilting up toward the front. I check it with a level and call Erica. My keyboard's slanting, I tell her; it's a whole "bubble" off level. She makes a note and calls back reassuringly; the technicians say it's designed that way.

Erica has told me about her family's "piano camp" in Bennington, Vermont. There's one in October; I should call for the information. You can go if you're a beginner;

you can go if you're a concert artist. I gather you can go if you've got the money.

I'm making some progress with the Miracle course. I've played "Dark Eyes," or in Russian, "Ochi Chernyi," described as a "dark, brooding love song," and learned about the key of A minor and about "accidentals"—sharps or flats that are written in front of the notes and apply only to those notes in that measure of music. Neenah proved to be a better teacher this week, though. I was stuck in a piece of music, couldn't get it to sound right; she walked by and looked at the screen and said, "B-flat there too." I was very embarrassed. B-flat was marked on the music, on the proper line in both the treble and the bass clef, and I had been playing those notes correctly. But then the music went below the staff in the bass into the next register, and I didn't realize *that* B would also be a flat. The computer had no way of knowing how stupid I was being. A teacher would have seen it quickly and said, "No, look, the B-flat in the key signature means *all* the Bs on the keyboard."

I liked playing the minor chords in "Dark Eyes" (the computer said, at Grand Finale time, "OK, let's play the famous 'Dark Eyes' as moodily as possible"). Then I was invited into the Practice Room, to try some of the new chord patterns in "Hava Nagila," "Mack the Knife," and "Yesterday." But there was a better Beatles' song waiting in Chapter 13.

"Here, There and Everywhere"—"In this chapter you will learn:

"—more fingering tricks

"—syncopation

"—two new E7 chords."

Syncopation is, by Miracle definition, "holding a note while the chord changes." I can play it, but I'm not sure I understand it.

It's a lovely song, with stately chord progressions, three at a time up the bass clef, and a melody in the right hand that could have come from a New York song-writer in the late 1940s; you wonder if Lennon and McCartney, writing in Liverpool in the sixties, had any idea how good they were. The tune has a satisfying end-ing, and then it's easy just to roll back into the opening and play it around again. My problem comes with the metronome. As you work through the phrases of a new song, the computer will ask you to play along with a metronome beat, slow at first, and then the whole song is to be played at the right tempo. The computer catches me trying to play too fast: "You misplayed most of the whole notes in the piece. Your most common problem with these notes was playing them too late." I get especially confused when I have to perform with the Miracle Orchestra: "You came in about 24 and a half beats late." There is a way to escape this. You move over into the Practice Room, select "Here, There and Every-where" in *notes only* mode, and you can play it at what-ever speed you like, without the ticking metronome. But still the computer makes you pay attention. There's an indicator bar—highlighting the music as you go along —that won't move forward until you've hit the right note.

Dr. John—whose music I've been hearing a lot of— just *throws* his hands at the keyboard. *Blap, blam, bippetybip, bop.* Our interview, about his autobiography and his latest CD, unfortunately took place at a distance: He was in New York, and I didn't get to watch him play or even shake his hand. His voice was soft, raspy New Orleans coming down the fiber-optic line from our New York studio. The original Dr. John was an old-time traveling medicine man. The new Dr. John, Mac Rebennack—a studio musician in need of a persona—borrowed the stage name in 1967. Mac Rebennack started young as a guitar player. He was taking lessons at age seven. When he was twelve, he'd sneak into the Canal Street clubs at 4:00 or 5:00 A.M.; the music would still be going on from the night before.

Rebennack had to switch from guitar after a fight at a motel on Christmas Eve 1961. The argument was about the motel owner's wife and another musician. A gun was fired, and Rebennack's finger was almost shot off.

DR. JOHN: Yeah, it kind of changed my gears about playing guitar for a while. I had my finger. They sewed it back on, but it was put in a big cast. And for a while I played drums and upright bass for a Dixieland band, which I was not really thrilled about because I never knew how to set up drums. And also carrying an upright bass around was not my idea of fun either. So that's what prompted me to get into hanging with James Booker and learning how to play the organ because it was right around the time when Jimmy Smith was getting popular and there was a lot of organ clubs around the country. And Booker taught me how to play a Hammond B-3 organ and that was basically my first keyboard gig.

NDA: If you go through your book, you find all the names from the decades of rock and roll, Eric Clapton, The Band, John Lennon. The only time you use the word *genius* is to describe James Booker. You reserve *genius* for James Booker alone.

DR. JOHN: Well, he was the only musician I ever met that I think could have been a true genius. And when he was fourteen years old and he was doing recording sessions, he'd come into the studio and play Bach fugues and play Haydn's stuff and could sit down and play "Malagueña Boogie," and all the real popular stuff of those days. And a guy that was in the band bought an alto sax and heard James Booker play it and gave James Booker the saxophone because he was so intimidated. The funny part was James Booker hadn't played a saxophone in years. I mean, *just picked it up and scared a cat that does that every night.* I remember a gig at the Aragon Ballroom in Chicago where he played a theater organ. And anybody who knows about a theater organ knows when you hit a note, the sound doesn't come out for a period of time after that. And he played the whole first part of a rhythm and blues–type gig on that organ. Hadn't played one of those since maybe the last time he had played in a church. But he did things that; you ask any of the cats from New Orleans who they might consider a genius, and they'll say James Booker.

NDA: And he died a very lonely death, I guess, at a pretty early age.

DR. JOHN: Well, he had developed eccentricisms toward the end of his life beyond, I think, anything he could rectify. He had lost an eye. He had lost his family. And just—the people who were close to him had all passed away, and it just pushed him over the edge.

NDA: Died of—in the end, a cocaine overdose?

DR. JOHN: Yes. And it was just so sad to see somebody go out that way.

NDA: That brings to mind a quotation from your book. I was a bit shocked to read this sentence: "In 1989"—this is near the end—"after thirty-four years of off-and-on but mostly on use of heroin, I began to get a handle on my addiction." And you suggest that all that time you had never really tried to quit, didn't think it was necessary.

DR. JOHN: Well, I wouldn't say I didn't try to quit. It was I didn't think I could, and it was something I used to have a horrible fear of what would take me out and put me six by six on this planet.

NDA: You say it was a nurse who one day brought you, in a rehab center in a hospital, a tangerine.

DR. JOHN: Yeah, I was about to go follow a nurse to where they were giving an old guy who was dying Demerol and morphine. I was going to follow her to the narcotic box. And this other nurse walked in the room and offered me a tangerine. And I don't know why it turned my life around with a tangerine, but it did. It worked.

NDA: When you look back and when you listen to the music you made over all these years, do you find that any of it was at all impaired by the addiction?

DR. JOHN: Well, I was what you call a functioning addict. I think the reason I got into that particular drug at that time, old-timers would show me how to function and work behind it. And it probably did impair a lot of things in my life, but not necessarily in the musical field. *Maybe* it did. But the one thing I have seen is the damage it caused to my family and people around me, my children, my grandchildren. Everything around me was hurt by that, and I'd had the one rationale in all those years that I wasn't hurting anybody but me. I learned that was a kind of jive, cleaning-up-my-act cop-out.

Then there's Tori Amos, a much younger piano star with an entirely different audience. She's a pop singer who's sold a million copies of one CD; she's a constant video presence on MTV and is taken seriously as a pianist, appearing on the cover of *Piano & Keyboard* magazine.

I'd heard she was coming to town. I went to a record store at lunchtime one day and bought a copy of her new CD, *Under the Pink*. At my next stop, an espresso place, the fellow behind the counter saw me reading the back cover of the CD and said, "Oh, Tori Amos, huh? Her concert just sold out; somebody here was there at noon and got a couple of tickets."

The Warner Theatre seats nineteen hundred; all the tickets went in an hour. They announced two additional concert nights, and those sold out quickly. Atlantic Records managed to find me a press ticket for the first night, a good seat about one-third of the way up in the middle front section.

If the Tori Amos audience was *one person,* it would be a seventeen-year-old girl, with well-faded torn jeans and boots and a tight shirt, curly hair, and a certain moist expression. When Tori Amos came out onstage, her fans in the audience saw themselves. But certainly a *hotter* version.

She strides out through the crossed purple spotlight beams. An intense, smoky red light pours down on the piano. There are six sound monitors facing her. She sits in a secure envelope of streaming light, her technical crew in the darkness behind her, the people who know all of her songs waiting in front. And Tori Amos touches the piano lightly; it's a Bösendorfer, beautifully miked. Big crunchy sounds from the bass; the nine-foot Bösendorfer grand has four extra bass keys. This will be all the music onstage tonight. By itself her piano can be a rock and roll band. And her voice: whispering and keening in your ear, songs of protest ("God—Sometimes You Just Don't Come Through") and confession and rapture. Tori Amos sits at the end of the piano bench, her *left* foot is on the sustain pedal, her right leg opens to the audience, she moves with her playing. One reviewer said, "It's like she's fucking the piano bench."

She was only slightly less intense in person the next morning when she came to our studio to talk and to play some. She bounced in happily, dusted her hands with face powder, and then splashed down the piano keys to make sure the sound was okay (after many years of having no piano, then later a small Baldwin, NPR now has two Schimmel grands).

Tori Amos is in her early thirties, and she's had a long career already, beginning in piano bars early in her teens. She was born in North Carolina, the daughter of a Methodist minister. Her parents soon moved to Baltimore so she could attend the Peabody Conservatory. It was clear almost from the time she was walking that she'd be a pianist:

MS. AMOS: Two and a half.
NDA: Two and a half?
MS. AMOS: That's what my mama says.

NDA: How were you able to just get up on a stool and play? Do you understand how that is?

MS. AMOS: I understand that this is like SpaghettiOs. I understand that it was a yummy feeling, that you crawl up and make friends with the sound.

NDA: And when you went to the conservatory, then, did that interfere with the way you heard music?

MS. AMOS: I was accepted at Peabody when I was five, and the whole idea was to get me to read. The problem with getting me to read was—it was so frustrating, because they started me on "Hot Cross Buns" and I could play scores of musicals by then. So, when you can play, you know, Rodgers and Hart, or Gershwin by ear, maybe not perfect, but, you know, you get the gist of "Summertime," then you're going, "Hang on a minute." From "Summertime" to "Hot Cross Buns" is a far cry. You're not seeing SpaghettiOs anymore. It's not yummy anymore. You know, twelve people doing this [plays a scale] as I'm walking down the hall, why do I want to be the thirteenth? I want to create my own thing.

NDA: You said in one interview, in *Rolling Stone*, I believe, that you are far more adventurous at the piano than you are in real life. What happens at the piano that doesn't happen to you out in the real world?

MS. AMOS: I don't feel guilty when I'm at the piano. I do understand that when I'm back in my hotel room, when I'm writing certain things about people that I've just met or run into, that I'm not really having certain relationships with them that I'm having at the piano. But at the piano all this is existing, and she and I are totally cohorts. We know exactly what we're creating, and this world is very real to me except when I'm onstage because that's like fantasy land for everybody. But it's just the opposite to me. Real life is really when I'm playing. Then it's off to the next gig.

NDA: Could it be any other instrument?

MS. AMOS: No.

NDA: Why?

MS. AMOS: The thing about this instrument is it's an orchestra, really. It's very much a warm, living, breathing woman to me. It's very female. She's my best friend. I sit and talk to her, curl up around her sometimes. It's a real being to me.

NDA: Could you be happy with a digital piano in any way?

MS. AMOS: No, no, of course not. There's no sustain. This is the biggest part of my sound, is that.

NDA: The right pedal there?

MS. AMOS: Yeah, this is the biggest part of everything I do. I play the sustain like it's a whole 'nother instrument [*demonstrates*]. Maybe I hold this for the entire tune. Electric pianos, also, they're not living, breathing things. I mean this is—it's all about the breath, the air.

The Tori Amos Under the Pink World Tour rolls on out of town. She takes the Bösendorfer piano along in a truck, and there's also a tuner in the road crew. It's got to ease the anxieties a bit to have the same trusty piano waiting in every new concert hall. Bösendorfer is an Austrian piano, dating back to 1828. The firm won the endorsement of Franz Liszt; he couldn't break the strings on the Bösendorfer pianos.

In the Second World War Allied bombs hit the Bösendorfer lumberyard, and artillery shells almost destroyed the factory. It's said that when the Russians occupied Vienna, soldiers broke the pianos up for firewood. The Bechstein piano company in Berlin and Blüthner in Leipzig also barely survived the war. Steinway in Hamburg came out a bit better. A factory building was bombed; there was damage to a warehouse storing new pianos, but Steinway was still a recognizable piano manufacturer at war's end.

In 1965 a German émigré named Franz Mohr became chief concert technician for Steinway & Sons in New York. He'd worked ten years for Steinway's Düsseldorf branch, as a tuner and concert manager. Franz Mohr came from a family of musicians. He wanted to be a violinist and enrolled in a conservatory in Cologne. In an essay in the book *The Lives of the Piano*, Dominique Browning relates what happened at that school:

> *One winter night in 1943 the American air force bombed the Hochschule für Musik in Cologne, Germany, where Franz Mohr was a student. Mohr ran from his house and by the time he got there, all the*

buildings were on fire. As he watched them burn, he heard the music that instruments make when they are dying. Instruments caved in with a wild jangle of sound. Piano strings screeched and snapped. In the concert hall an organ burst into flames. As hot air rushed through the organ's pipes, it began to bellow and wail. The sound of it has haunted Mohr ever since.

MAY

John Grisham? I've met him. He's rich. Bet he can't play the piano

TURNS OUT THERE'S NO TIME THIS SPRING FOR A TRIP DOWN to western Virginia and over into the Allegheny Mountains to visit our friends Anne and Donald McCaig. Donald's a writer and often tapes essays for *All Things Considered*. They don't come much to Washington, and it's hard for us to get there; we live a good day's drive apart.

I'm usually reminded of the McCaigs and their farm and their dogs when I'm in a shopping mall. I go in grudgingly, knowing I can't last long. The floors seem slick, skittery. There's a scary, cacophonous swirl of music and sound, and people look overfed and a touch evil; everyone's wearing stonewashed jeans and big white basketball shoes. I get close to what I'm looking for, a pair of shoes, a book, but I can tell my eyes are starting to dart about, and there's a taste of copper in my mouth. Perhaps it's the air—an invisible chemical mist from thousands of newly made socks, sweaters and boom boxes and washing machines. "Let's go," I'll ask Neenah. She's thinking, *We've just been here ten minutes*, but knows the feeling herself so we're quickly in the car and off for a swim at the Y or a fruit-smoothie drink from a nearby organic café. Whatever's fresh: papaya, kiwi, apples, coconut milk. It seems calming, restorative. And then I think of the McCaigs' farm, at close to two thousand feet in Highland County, along the Cowpasture River. There is a theory developing in science called the Biophilia Hypothesis. Biologist Edward O. Wilson suggested that humans have a genetically based need to be close to the natural world. And that if we live in cities, we are disconnected from the vitality of nature; we need trees, open water, a range of hills. Just imagining the drive down through the high valley where the McCaigs live makes me feel better.

Neenah and I will talk from time to time about what sort of life we could have in a place as far away as Highland County. We probably wouldn't be farming. There's a lovely small town there called Monterey, and on my frustrated nights I realize I could almost buy a house in Monterey for what I paid for this piano. Buy the nice old white frame house, move down there, take along a fax machine and computer and tape recorders, and then figure out how to make enough money to get by.

And surely there's music enough in life without having to pay big money for it. Donald and Anne McCaig both sing to their dogs every day. They have Border collies to help work the sheep. Pip was one of their first dogs and a treasured friend. Donald would ruffle Pip's fur and sing:

Oh, ho, where have you been,
   Pippy-boy, Pippy-boy?
Oh, ho, where have you been,
   charming Pippy?
I have been to the State Fair
   and I won a ribbon there!
I'm a young dog and cannot leave my faarrr-m.

Border collies are not overly affectionate and would not be sentimental, but these dogs know they have their own songs, and they want to hear them every day. Silk's tune is from "I'm a Little Teapot."

I'm a little Silky, short and stout.
   Here is my tailpiece,
   here is my snout.

When you roll me over,
   I will shout:

"Please don't throw this good
dog out."

So instead of traveling, Neenah and I stay close to
home, and on a rainy Sunday evening we light a fire and
sit on the couch to watch a video documentary about
Vladimir Horowitz. THE GREATEST PIANIST DEAD OR ALIVE,
a newspaper headline said in 1928, when Horowitz
came to America and started playing concerts. In the
documentary we see him when he is in his seventies and
eighties—playing with an absolute concentration and
with strong, confident hands. The notes trill and dance,
and in the louder sections his fingers seem to flash and
grow instantly longer to reach the difficult notes. His
wife, Wanda, who is Arturo Toscanini's daughter, sits
with Mr. Horowitz in their New York apartment, and
they speak of his time of depression—twelve years, between 1953 and 1965. Perhaps a nervous breakdown.
He didn't leave the house for two years; for the first year
he didn't leave his room. Horowitz says of this time, "I
was very happy," and points out that he did start making records again. Recordings made not in the studio
but right in the apartment. His return to public performance was in Carnegie Hall. He and his wife bought
coffee and doughnuts for those waiting for tickets. The
concert was a triumph.

Wanda explains that she was always attracted by his
playing. "What kept us together was the music. I also
liked him as a person." They were married almost fifty-

six years. In the documentary she is shown *listening* to her husband play in the apartment. She preferred to stand outside the room, in the hallway by the stairs. "I listen here because I don't see him, I'm not under the spell, the magic spell."

In 1986 Vladimir Horowitz made a homecoming trip to the Soviet Union. He had been a precocious young star when he'd left Russia, eager to test his playing in Berlin, Rome, London, New York. This would be his first time back, and his last. He goes to Moscow, and his piano goes with him. It is hoisted out of the window of his Upper East Side apartment, taken to Steinway for packing, then sent on to the airport. His tuner goes along to Russia as well. Horowitz says: "I never go without Franz Mohr going wherever I go, to properly prepare the piano for me right there."

It is a moment of heroism for the Russian people, who have waited longer than a half century for Horowitz to return. The stage is lit with the glow of pride from the audience. At the end of the evening, Horowitz finishes three short Chopin selections, stands, smiles—there's an explosion of applause and cheers of "bravo"—and walks off the stage before his encore. At his return he begins a quiet and dreamy piece. Clearly it's music the audience knows well. The camera stays on the face of a stalwart gray-haired man; a tear falls down his cheek. A young girl is shown, face lifted to the stage. Dark hair, white blouse, her eyes shining. There is a soft cascade of piano notes, slowing to silence. Vladimir

Horowitz, eighty-two years old, makes a small, slight gesture, lifting his open hands to say: "It's the best I can do," and wipes his nose with a handkerchief.

Neenah and I watch, wondering, how can a piece of music mean this much? Just a few minutes long, and simple. I wasn't sure of the title when it was shown for a second on the screen just as Horowitz was beginning, so we wait to check the program credits. It is "Träumerei," by Robert Schumann. It sounded like something *I* could play, I thought. Surely given enough time and some teaching, I could at least find the notes.

At NPR the next day there's planning for a trip to Mississippi. Our program is doing a series of stories about welfare in America, and we've found that Mississippi has an adult education program that seems to be working. The state provides high school equivalency training by satellite television. I've always wanted to go to Oxford, and I mention that John Grisham lives there. "Talk to him too," says Ellen Weiss, our executive producer, and a Grisham fan, "it'll be a great trip." I haven't read much of his work; my book interviews tend to be with the sorts of writers who would be shocked to see someone reading their books on an airplane. But I liked the movie *The Pelican Brief,* and we just watched *The Firm* at home this spring. It has a great score, solo piano music, written and played by Dave Grusin, and nicely recorded. A phone call to John Grisham's editor. Yes, he'll talk with you. He has a new book coming out. *The Chamber;* it's about death row.

After a flight down to Memphis and an hour's drive south, I'm sitting in an Oxford restaurant called the City Grocery, eating shrimp and cheese grits with my producer and an engineer. After dinner we walk next door to Square Books, one of the best independent bookstores in the country. Nanci Griffith's recording of Dylan's "Boots of Spanish Leather" is playing on the sound system, lots of people in the store in the evening. Square Books has fourteen-foot ceilings downstairs, and an outdoor balcony upstairs, overlooking the county courthouse, which is painted white with a four-sided clock tower. On a misty night you might imagine a slight white-haired figure walking past. Everyone in this town has William Faulkner stories—"Mr. Bill" they called him.

And they are truly proud of John Grisham. He went to law school here, practiced nearby, lives outside town now in a big house, coaches Little League baseball, and shows up every week to teach Sunday school. His income from books and movies is perhaps ten million dollars a year.

And—I notice the next morning when Grisham arrives for the interview—you can *see* a good deal of that money. He's wearing a blue shirt and khaki pants, loafers with no socks. He moves with an athlete's confidence. As I wrote later, "John Grisham looks like a man who has a chance to work out every day and time to take a nap."

We have arranged to do the interview at Square

Books, upstairs, with two chairs by a window. His editor had been strict: "You must be ready to start taping as soon as John walks in the door at ten A.M." (apparently he's been frustrated by waiting for TV crews to get the lighting right). But he was on time, in a good mood, and as soon as he sat down, he was trying hard, answering the same old questions with fresh anecdotes. (He was genuinely pleased to learn that we had both read—as kids growing up—the Chip Hilton series of books about a high school sports star.)

We talk some about *The Chamber* and talk a lot about his first book, *A Time to Kill.* It was written in longhand, on legal pads, mostly in the mornings. He told me: "I'd get up at five and get to the office and try to have the first cup of coffee made and sit at my desk and write the first word at five-thirty. And a lot of times I did it, and that's the only way the book got written, was the early-morning stuff."

He'd write a page or two during the day if he had to wait thirty minutes for a judge to show up. The book needed three years of his spare time, went through nine different drafts, and then it didn't sell. Dozens of publishers turned it down. Finally there was an agent who liked it and an editor who took a chance, but as *A Time to Kill* was being sold, Grisham was already making himself a different sort of writer. He'd begun work on *The Firm* and now understood how to put together a plot-driven novel. He'd analyzed the novels on the bestseller list. He saw how fast the plot had to turn the pages and understood that character development could slow down the action. The new books are far less literary, less writerly than the first one was. *A Time to Kill,* though, remains his own favorite. And of course, after he became famous, people wanted to read it; the book that almost wasn't published has now sold more than nine million copies.

I ask Grisham about how he's handling the fame; by some measurements he's the most successful writer of all time. He says he does sometimes think about disappearing, but he figures Oxford is still the best place to live; people protect him here; the town's been through it all before, with William Faulkner. Then Grisham tells a "famous writer's" story: "Stephen King and I were eating breakfast at Smitty's around the corner here two weeks ago, and he said he'd saved all his cholesterol for this trip. And so we were having grits and bacon and eggs and homemade biscuits with gravy, and this guy at the next table yelled at me and wanted to know the baseball score from last night. And Stephen King says, 'Who is that?' And I say, 'Chuckie Faulkner.' He said, 'As in Mr. Bill?' I said, 'Mr. Bill was his uncle.' And he said, 'That guy over there is Faulkner's nephew? I just can't believe it: I'm eating sawmill gravy and grits, and there's Faulkner's nephew over there.' And he was blown away by it."

My allotted hour's interview time is up. And now

several young women have gathered in the bookstore, waiting downstairs to meet John Grisham. They will also say hello to his wife, who's come to collect him.

In the evening our crew accepts an invitation from the bookstore's owners, Richard Howarth and his wife, Lisa, and we all get in the back of a Chevy Silverado pickup truck and ride out into the warm Mississippi dusk to eat catfish at a country store by the railroad tracks. We're riding with Anne Rapp. It's her truck, with a Texas license plate, though she usually works out of Los Angeles. Anne is a script supervisor for the movies. She worked on *The Firm* shoot in Memphis, with director Sydney Pollack. On the single weekend they had off she drove down to see Oxford—the university, William Faulkner's home, Square Books. It was her dream to write fiction, and she decided to really give it a try—bought the Silverado, turned down the next few movie offers, found a small house to rent in Oxford, and talked her way into a class in creative writing at the university.

We've found nice rooms in a bed-and-breakfast close by the campus, and after catfish and hush puppies, I'm looking fondly toward a good night's sleep. Some of the others are going out to a music club to hear Pinetop Perkins play blues. "He won't be around much longer," they said, but I don't recognize the name and I'm tired and need to make some notes about the morning's interview with John Grisham. You can think of his story as a super example of adult education. He was in his thirties, doing okay as a lawyer, but started to believe he could be a writer. You just try to figure things out, and you make a commitment; you don't do it halfway. It's what happened with Anne Rapp and her chance at fiction writing. It could be the same thing with my piano —if I'd create a way to have both time and focus. But as I fall asleep in Oxford, Mississippi, I am really more envious of Anne's Silverado shortbed 350-V8 with a toolbox on the back than I am of her new start. I'd like to have that truck *and* my new piano. At least I could drive the truck.

In the morning I find out that Pinetop Perkins is a "legendary piano player," but he was sick last night, they said, and only his band showed up at the club. It bothers me that I didn't know who he was.

Back in Washington, riding home from work on the subway, I'm trying to think of ways to get back to Mississippi for some more stories. There are several civil rights anniversaries coming up soon. And when I get to the house, Neenah is at the piano trying to find the notes for "Nkosi Sikelel' iAfrika," the song that has now become South Africa's national anthem. We've been hearing it on radio and television, as the African National Congress celebrates victory in that country's first one-person, one-vote election. She's playing the melody pretty well, from memory; we'll have to look for the sheet music.

I'd also like to learn "We Shall Overcome." You could play it just in chords, as a hymn. "Oh, deep in my heart/I do believe/we shall overcome someday." It would be quiet and powerful on the piano; maybe the beginning piano books should include the songs that really mean something. This one is a spiritual that became a Baptist hymn and then, in 1945, a union song. It was sung on the picket line during a Food and Tobacco Workers strike in South Carolina. Two of the Charleston union women brought it to a workshop at the Highlander Folk School in East Tennessee, a training center for labor organizers, and later civil rights workers. Pete Seeger learned the song at Highlander in 1947 and changed "We will overcome" to "We *shall* overcome." As the struggle grew in the South, the song became more widely known; it was heard at rallies and sit-in demonstrations. I've heard it sung myself at the Highlander Center, during a workshop on music as an organizing tool. And a workshop leader told the story of the night in 1959 when Highlander was raided by county and state police. Tennessee authorities believed the school was a "meeting place for known Communists" and knew that blacks and whites could be found attending workshops together. The police went in, ostensibly looking for illegal whiskey. Several of the Highlander staff were taken away for resisting arrest. The lights were out inside the center; many people were frightened. Someone started to whistle "We Shall Overcome." Others started singing, and the song gained a new verse: "We are not afraid."

May stays chilly, wet. We light fires if we're home

together in the evening and keep thinking each one will be the last. At four o'clock on a Saturday afternoon the peonies begin to open—sweet-smelling luminous red blossoms. We'll have white ones too, a bit later, with creamy yellow centers. And the lilies of the valley—my grandmother's favorite—are also blooming, alongside the brick walls where they get plenty of sun. We sleep with the bedroom window open, to hear the mourning doves just at sunrise and for the smell of lilies in the cold air at night.

These are long days of work for both of us. Neenah's finishing the sound track for Discovery's Normandy invasion program. She's trying to help make the silent archival black-and-white footage come alive (one night she wrapped a can of tomato soup in a towel and banged it lightly against the big copper-wound bass strings of the piano, recording the effect to see if it might help with the sound of explosions). And I'm working on *All Things Considered* every day plus trying to write the stories about John Grisham and Mississippi's adult literacy program. Seven days can speed right past us without much notice, and I'll realize I haven't spent any time at the piano. I make promises to play first thing in the morning, but the snooze button gets me in trouble, and then I'll hear something interesting on the radio and I'll have to start reading the *New York Times* and the *Washington Post.* The day starts running away. At night, after a beer, after dinner, my mind seems blurry and my hands are clumsy.

To push myself just a little, I send off a fifty-dollar check to David Sudnow, in Princeton, New Jersey. In response to an ad in the paper: DAVID SUDNOW WON'T GIVE YOU WEEKLY PIANO LESSONS. HE DOESN'T HAVE TO. (I interviewed Sudnow several years ago about his teaching ideas.) The ad continues: "He's found a faster way. With an exciting two day course. Learn to play favorite songs by ear, with a full, professional sound. In months. Not years. For beginners and those with training, the results are astounding." That's good enough for me, so I mail off the deposit for a seminar coming up in New York, on a weekend in June. SPACE IS LIMITED. RESERVE A SEAT TODAY.

I suppose, though, I can deal with a quiet, simple piece of music here at home. I'm up to Lesson 16 in the Miracle course, and it's Pachelbel's "Canon in D." I'm pleased to see it. One of my favorite folk songs, "The Streets of London," borrows from this work. And Pachelbel's "Canon" was featured on the sound track of the movie *Ordinary People*. It's a lovely melody that isn't hurt by becoming so popular. (It's Johann Pachelbel, my music encyclopedia tells me. Organist and composer, Nuremberg, Germany, 1653–1706.) The Miracle screen tells me: "Listen now to the famous Pachelbel 'Canon.'" Sounds easy, just single notes in the treble and the bass, played together. I have to learn "A Finger-crossing" to play this: The right thumb moves to tuck away inside the hand, and the index finger crosses over to reach for a key farther down; it's a way to cover more space on the keyboard and still have the notes be connected. The "Canon"—the Miracle edition—is only eight notes for each hand. They are played in unison, six descending notes, then two going back up; then the melody repeats. And repeats. You could play it as a meditation. I do get a little dreamy working on it, and when it's time to perform with the Miracle Orchestra, I freeze up as the accompaniment starts: Harpsichord harmonies are provided, flute overlays, an electric piano percussion. I just sit and listen and watch the note indicator moving along the score, showing me what I should be playing. When the music's over, the Miracle responds petulantly: "It was your turn to play the piece! You didn't play anything. Your overall performance was 0%. Your pitch performance was 0%. And your rhythm performance was 0%."

Looking for a brighter mood, I move on to "The Entertainer"; the Scott Joplin tune is the basis for Lesson 17. It's another made-famous-by-movies song—from the Robert Redford-Paul Newman picture *The Sting*. And here we learn "A Thumbcrossing." The idea again is to move the hand more easily up the keyboard. The well-known opening notes of "The Entertainer": The thumb plays D; the second finger plays D sharp as the thumb reaches underneath for E; then the hand has plenty of reach for the high C.

I stay with this song, practicing both in the mornings and before bedtime. The Miracle has a "Parachute Jump" to help me master the left-hand chords. A helicopter flies onto the screen. The chords appear on a bass stave. Three paratroopers get set to jump. If I play the chord correctly, their chutes open and they float to the ground. If I mess up, they jump anyway; the chutes stay closed, and they land with a thud and a grunt. I can tolerate this game once or twice, for training, but if I'm making mistakes as I go along in the practice, the Miracle screen will say, "You need some more work. Let's go back to the Parachute Range," and I'll refuse, clicking the mouse to move on to the next lesson segment. Also, I'm having my usual difficulties with time. I don't seem to have enough patience to appreciate the precise value of the notes. The "Miracle Quiz Time" has me confounded: "How many 8th note beats in a dotted half note?" I can choose 3, 4, 6, or 8. I click-guess 4. "Blaaaat," the computer says. I venture to click 8. "Blaaaat." 6? I wonder. "*Yes.*" The Miracle issues a pleased bong sound.

But I am learning the "rag" rhythm, and there is indeed a swinging feel to the music that comes easily. I practice the right hand, then the left hand, then both hands together. Play it slowly, add the ticking metronome, play it faster, trying to increase to performance tempo. After a week of steady practice, though, I can't make it, can't play it that fast. I peek ahead to the end of the lesson. If you play "The Entertainer" at the proper speed, Miracle is ready to say: "Nice work. That song had both a complex rhythm and some very tricky fingerings."

Scott Joplin was very concerned about the way this music would be played. He wrote a manual called *The School of Ragtime*, urging careful study: "That real ragtime of the higher class is rather difficult to play is a painful truth which most pianists have discovered. . . . To assist amateur players in giving the 'Joplin Rags' that weird and intoxicating effect intended by the composer is the object of this work." He cautions the beginner: "Play slowly until you catch the swing, and never play ragtime fast at any time." And I find a Joshua Rifkin recording of "The Entertainer" (the song is not among the three Joplin-performed piano rolls that survive). It does sound slow—and glorious! The treble part is full of chiming, happy notes. Each phrase seems a celebration. It's discouraging to compare this recording to the small arrangement I've just been learning; Rifkin's version of "The Entertainer" is a graceful ship under sail, passing on the horizon. Mine is a clunky rowboat, messing about in the harbor.

I get out for a Saturday morning 8K race, right in the neighborhood. The 8:00 A.M. start time feels way too early. The race organizers were concerned about the heat, this far into May, but we have a clear, cool morning, and I've had just the right amount of coffee (plus one piece of toast with honey at 6:30). One of my *ATC* colleagues is running; another has volunteered to help out at the start. We're off and down Wisconsin Avenue, a straight line and mostly flat for two miles. We pass a Starbucks, and it's tempting to stop and have coffee and just sit and read the papers. A turn down to Massachusetts Avenue as we head back north. The police hold back the traffic at intersections, but sometimes there's an angry driver, honking. I get a nice chilly, tingly feeling at the three-mile mark (a volunteer stands with a stopwatch, calling out the elapsed times). It's a sensation that, for me, happens only in a race; I just don't run fast enough in practice. I sprint the last half mile; people near the finish line are cheering, "Lookin' good. You can do it." I grin like a sixth-grade kid breaking the string at a track meet.

I love the endorphin flush this kind of running brings. My friends and I swagger around, drinking Evian and orange juice, our free race T-shirts over our shoulders, talking about our finishing times. I'm a slow runner—about nine minutes a mile—but it's the best, cheapest fun I know about.

Neenah calls in from Bedford, Virginia, a tiny town at the edge of the Blue Ridge Mountains. She's been doing interviews about the town's young men who went ashore at Normandy with the U.S. Army's 29th Division; this is for an *ATC* story coming up on Memorial Day. She's met some friendly and interesting people, found good food at the Town and Country restaurant, and even has had time to go hiking.

Our dogs, Will and Bonny, get restless when Neenah's away. The windows are open, and there's a cool breeze tonight. They can hear other dogs barking out in the neighborhood, and they answer them, holding their heads high and still as they listen, then yelping in response. It's like the Disney movie *One Hundred and One Dalmatians*. We've also had a dog visitor. He came with Donald McCaig, who's in town for a bookstore appearance; he has a new novel called *Nop's Hope*. We stopped in for his reading and the signing. Harry, one of the McCaigs' working Border collies, stayed by Donald's feet at the bookstore and spent the night in the front seat of the car in our driveway. The next morning Harry had a good backyard romp before they headed home to Highland County.

Donald slept in a spare bed we'd put up in the office, next to the piano. I'd told him I was trying to learn. He didn't ask me to play; that wouldn't be his nature. But in our copy of his new book I notice he's written, "For my friends, Noah & Neenah—they laughed when I sat down at the piano."

JUNE

The attack of the humidity monster and a songwriter's million-selling moment

A WOMAN WITH A TOOL KIT IS AT THE DOOR. CAROL, THE piano tuner, arrives early on a hot morning for the free tuning included with the Steinway purchase. She's called a couple of times, but I've been putting it off. I just don't seem to have a connection with this piano. I've got the Miracle keyboard set up on a small table next to my desk, and that's where my learning time goes. "Be careful about that," a knowledgeable friend has warned. "You might be learning music with that computer, but you're not learning how to *play*, and it's hard to go back to the piano after those keyboards."

Carol is friendly and fast. She lifts back the piano's lid. Larry Fine, a Boston technician and author of *The*

Piano Book, mentions this moment: "If you store the Harvard University library, museum and arboretum on your piano, please clear them off before the technician arrives. You won't believe how much stuff people pile on their pianos." Carol lifts *off* the vertical front panel, popping it out of its fasteners, exposing the hammers and the tuning pins. She has a small electronic tuning meter that will precisely confirm what she already knows from just walking into the room. "This piano's in big trouble," she says. "You've got the window open there, and the humidity's high. All these strings here in the middle are way too sharp." She plays a few notes, and of course I can hear it now: The notes are metallic and whiny and sound brittle; no wonder the piano hasn't been pleasant to play lately. Carol says, "Strings start *breaking* at this tension in pianos in Baptist churches in the summertime." The problem is simple: Wood swells. A piano's soundboard—delicate, resonant, usually made of spruce—will gather moisture from the air and expand upward. The strings are arrayed across bridges above the soundboard, but the bridges are glued to the sound-board so as the humidity rises, so do the strings—and they start stretching. Tighter strings, higher pitch. Along about the first of December the whole business goes the other way: Strings loosen and the pitch falls.

There's not much Carol can do. She moves up and down the keyboard, tapping notes, making small adjust-ments with her tuning crank. She writes on the work order: "Piano is 22 cents sharp [the distance from one note to the next is divided into one hundred spaces, called cents]. In a room with an open window. High humidity is at dangerous levels. Strongly recommend a dehumidifier for piano room."

"It's a good instrument," Carol says, sitting on the bench after she's packed up her tools. She plays a verse of "Smile," and the piano tries to respond. "I think it'll be okay." But the humidity has to come down. There's a device called the Dampp-Chaser that fits inside the piano; it's a heating rod that acts as a dehumidifier. The system is controlled by a humidistat. Carol likes the Dampp-Chaser but says I need more drastic help—and fast.

At the hardware store on Saturday I decide on a General Electric dehumidifier. It's a big forty-pint unit. I take it home and start it running. The window is now shut. The humidity in the room—according to my gauge—is 92 percent. I turn out the lights and shut the door.

Two hours later the humidity has dropped to 80, and the room feels better, if a bit hot. The dehumidifier's water tank is filling up.

Three hours more, though, and I realize I've created a monster. The humidity is now 60, but since the exhaust fan on the dehumidifier noisily kicks out heat, the temperature is above *ninety*. The room is unlivable. The air is hot, sickly, desiccated. Nothing could be learned here, and music would not work. The humidity outside stays terribly high. At sunset there's thunder and high winds with splashes of dark rain. The dogs howl. Neenah's away this weekend, and the dogs and I have managed to discourage ourselves nicely.

But Sunday morning brings cooler air. I go to the farmer's market for lettuce, beets, and sugar snap peas. The Orioles are winning big in the afternoon. I decide to take the dehumidifier to the basement and plug it in; it's always far too damp down there, and the dogs will appreciate it. From storage in the attic I bring down an air conditioner and put it in the window ten feet away from my moist piano. The air will be cooler, appreciably drier, and, best of all, we can keep the room at a consistent temperature. To make all this work out, I have to construct a new window opening in the kitchen for Sally, the cat, since we're closing up her favorite entryway, but it's an easy project—only three more trips to the hardware store.

The ideal place for a piano, I'm now understanding, is a room in a totally air-conditioned, climate-controlled house. The Steinway owner's literature does make mention of potential problems with humidity, but surely no one at Steinway & Sons in New York is going to say: "Now hold on there! Before you buy this piano, we want some assurances about the relative humidity of your house."

I'm thankful that I didn't buy one of the really expensive grands; it would be awful to have thirty thousand dollars in a piano you couldn't keep tuned. In *The Piano Book* Larry Fine tells of being called to work on a grand that the owner claimed was going in and out of tune at different times during the day. Fine tried to tune the piano but noticed the pitch indeed did start to shift —just as the sunlight through a window began to shine directly on the soundboard. He closed the blinds; the piano came back into tune. And Jim Anderson, who records jazz albums in New York, has told me of noticing the pitch of a piano change as a high-pressure system passes through Manhattan. He'll be deep in a dark, quiet studio with the piano telling him how the weather's doing outside. Also, the thought occurs: If you had an electronic keyboard, you wouldn't even be thinking about any of these problems.

I decide to live with what I've got. The air conditioner seems to help. I dust the piano and open the top and the tilting front panel so the sound is more expansive, and you can see the white felt hammers and the brass and steel strings. I take the green felt covers off the pedals; they're tied on with red cords, and it's all a bit too cute anyway. One of the piano delivery guys said some people just leave the covers on until they fray and tatter away.

It's hard to know if this is the piano I'll have after twenty years; it's just too soon. I know I'd prefer the action of a grand; it's smoother and quicker. And with the vertical piano all the sound seems to splash right out in your face; with the grand the music stays under your fingers. But this 1098 seems a trusty little piano for now, pleasing under less-than-ideal circumstances.

I've been worried that I'm more interested in pianos than I am in music, worried that I spent a lot of time trying to decide about a particular model of piano and no time trying to find the right piano teacher. But in some cases there *is* just one certain, special instrument. I have the sheet music for "From a Distance" in my piano bench. It's the EASY PIANO arrangement, and I can play a little of it. "From a Distance": words and music by Julie Gold, and she's shown smiling, grinning really, on the cover of the music. A small young woman, brown hair, black jeans and a bright red jacket. She's sitting at an open piano, and perched just above her left shoulder is a small gold model of an old Victrola, the windup phonograph with the trumpet speaker horn. It's a Grammy award. Julie's song has sold millions worldwide. It was a big hit for Bette Midler; the version I like is by Nanci Griffith.

" 'From a Distance' was brewing in me for a long time," Julie says on the phone. "I really believe, without sounding creepy, that some songs you cowrite with God. Here's what happened just prior to writing it: I was twenty-nine, just about to turn thirty. I had been on a jury; we had to convict a man. He had attempted to kill somebody. He was guilty, but he had done what he thought he had to do. He thought *he* was going to be killed, he couldn't solve the problem any other way. The police took him to the emergency room, and the guy he had shot was lying there on the table. He's shot, but he still turns his head and looks up and makes a motion like he's slitting his throat, like 'I'm still gonna kill you.' So all these things were happening, justice and the American way, my brother was about to get married, I was a bubbling cauldron of emotion.

"For my thirtieth birthday my parents sent me the family piano. Do you know what it is to love your instrument? I had moved to New York to make it as a musician, but I didn't take the piano. For ten years I lived in New York, and I had a Wurlitzer electric piano. I hated it. To play the thing, I had to become an electrician and a mechanic, but it was all I had, and I needed it.

"So on my birthday the real piano came. I was a secretary at HBO; I *never* took the day off. It was a beautiful day, and for the first time I saw the piano outside in the glistening sunlight. It was a crystal-clear, freezing cold winter day on a street in Greenwich Village. The piano came down on a lift, and in five seconds it was in the house. I lived on the first floor, and they put it in place, and there we were—united. They said it's been on the truck twenty-four hours, and I had to let it rest; I wasn't allowed to play it. It was like being reunited with your loved one who has been in a Siberian work camp and then the Iron Curtain goes down and you aren't allowed to touch each other. I polished it and looked at it from my bed, which was a loft bed up over the piano. And I looked down at the piano all night—from a distance. The next day I came down from my bed and sat down and these majestic notes came out—the chords to 'From a Distance.' "

Julie's piano was a Knight upright, made in England. It has quite a good reputation. "The Beatles used to play a Knight," she says. She still has the Knight, but she's also bought a Steinway grand—five feet, ten and a half inches, made in 1917; it's the piano in the picture. It was rebuilt, restored really by Faust Pianos, a small firm in Irvington, New York.

Steinway & Sons today is competing with its past glory; the company has made two hundred thousand grand pianos, and most of them are still around, sounding great, or with the potential to sound great. It can be a delicate decision, trying to figure out how much work an older Steinway truly needs. "Don't touch it unless it's falling apart" is advice you can often hear. A *complete* restoration is possible: building a new piano around the old wooden shell and the original cast-iron plate. Larry Fine writes:

> Since the average life of a piano is around fifty years, and with proper restoration at least fifty more, it's silly to waste our resources buying new pianos when old ones can be so effectively recycled. Some used pianos have exquisite veneers, leg styles, carved cases, and ivory keys unavailable today on new pianos.

*Many of the companies that produce new pianos to-
day are huge conglomerates that turn out pianos by
the thousands in far away cities. How much more
satisfying to contribute to your local small-scale econ-
omy by buying a used piano that has been restored to
usefulness by local craftspeople.*

Faust Pianos is finishing three and a half new/old pianos a week. If you happened upon, say, a 1905 Steinway Model B seven-foot grand that's been sitting in a
closed-up parlor in an old house and hasn't been played
for decades and in fact won't make piano sounds anymore, you could call Sara Faust in Irvington and she'd
buy it for about seven thousand dollars. The same piano
four months later: the wood glowing, the ivory keys
shining, the tone deep and clear—more than thirty-
three thousand dollars. And she says you'd very likely
prefer this 1905 B to a brand-new one on the Steinway
showroom floor, selling for at least ten thousand dollars
more. She's been a concert pianist. "I have a new B here
in my shop," she says. "It has a lovely tone, but when I
want to sit down and play, I prefer the sound, the soul
of an old B that we've rebuilt."

Faust Pianos tries to find material to match what
Steinway used in the early 1900s. It has strings custom-
made in Canada; it's using "super-prime" Sitka spruce
for the new soundboards. And Sara Faust says, "It's difficult to find good hammer sets; a lot depends on the
kind of sheep the wool came from to make the felt for

the hammers. You'd be shocked to see how important that is. And then you still have to do a lot of work on them."

Faust says the heart of a piano is the cast-iron plate, and she's most fond of the older ones, made by Steinway in New York until the early 1940s. The company no longer operates its own foundry. In "the vintage years," the Steinway plates were hand-poured by craftsmen who had served long apprenticeships. And for her, the pianos built around those plates had a warmth that's unmatched by any piano built today.

The best Steinways—Sara Faust believes—were built between 1885 and 1930. The pianos of the 1950s still had a "distinctive, appealing sound," but then the tone started getting "icier." "In the old days," she says, "nine out of ten Steinway pianos would be great ones. Now it's one out of ten."

Could you build a piano in America that would compete with Steinway for the high end of the market? Part of the answer can be found in an old six-story-high red-brick factory building close by the B & M Diner (now empty) and the railroad tracks and the Merrimack River in Haverhill, Massachusetts. Once shoes were made in this building, but now it is a piano factory. And a very quiet one. It's shut down because of financial problems.

I have come to see the Falcone piano. I'd heard vague mentions of this brand and noticed a credit for the piano in the liner notes on a Butch Thompson recording made at Bluejay Studio in Carlisle, Massachusetts ("A wonderful Falcone 7′3″ grand, tuned by Jim Corkindale"). I thought I might see some piano *making* as well, and the factory certainly stands ready: Sunlight shines through the windows on trimmed stacks of white spruce and Vermont maple; the saws are waiting, the planers and sanders, a sandblasting machine. There are huge, curved presses with cranks on the sides to form the new piano cases. There's a special room where THE POUNDER lives. Bring the finished piano in here, and put it under the row of air compressor–driven hammers, and the machine starts playing. The idea is to loosen up the action, have the felt start to soften on the strings. It's a four-hour process, the pounding of all the keys producing a determined, disturbing music. The room is soundproofed.

Wood becomes pianos in this factory building in a vertical process. The wood is delivered to the ground floor, where it is cut, and moved higher and higher as it is smoothed and glued. It gathers brass and steel and plastic and paint from floor to floor and arrives in a loft with a view of Haverhill's once-busy industrial downtown. And here, in large, clean bays, the pianos would sit open to the touch of the regulators, for final adjustments to the action. In the last five years two craftsmen from Russia have been among those working on this quiet sixth floor, making the pianos musical.

Santi Falcone started this company in 1984. He thought he could build a better piano than Steinway. He wanted a piano that was more *expensive* than Steinway's. He made three models, all grands, all very close to the Steinway designs. Soon Falcone was selling more pianos than he could build, and he moved into this old, large factory and sold some stock to finance the expansion. It was a labor-intensive piano to build, doing it Santi Falcone's way. Six hundred fifty, even seven hundred hours of work, plus close supervision, to finish each instrument. Sales were strong, but even more money was needed; in 1989 Falcone had to sell out to his principal stockholder, and he chose to leave the company. The new management decided to concentrate on resurrecting the old and respected Mason & Hamlin piano designs, at a price *below* Steinway, and the Falcone became available only by special order, a "job shop piano." The Mason & Hamlin company, despite efforts to modernize and cut some of the labor hours out of the pianos, also ran into money troubles. And suffered through two fires, one doing two million dollars in damage. Both fires started in the paint shop, where the high-gloss lacquers are applied.

Production slowed and then stopped. Only a few people are around when I visit. The company's president, Allen Harrah, has time to walk through the plant with me. There is one completed piano left in the building. It is a Falcone concert grand, shiny black and big. The action needs some work, Allen explains: water damage from one of the fires. It looks and sounds fine, though. Allen goes into his office to take a call from someone who he thinks might want to buy this company—he's also expecting one of the Asian piano companies might be interested—and I sit and play the Falcone. The lid is propped all the way up—"full stick." There's a light, marvelous feeling to the keyboard and a mature richness to the tone. Allen comes back, and we trade places. He plays, "a little," he says, and rolls through some Rachmaninoff phrases. He plays the left-hand chords alone. "This is what this piano does so well. Hear how the bass notes are separate?" And you *can* notice the fat, cleanly distinct low notes. "My Steinway at home won't do this," Allen says. He has a sad shake of his head for the Falcone pianos, past and future.

Peter Mohr was the plant manager here for several years, adding a touch of Steinway heritage. Peter is the son of Franz Mohr, who was Steinway's chief technician and Horowitz's favorite tuner. Peter spent his school vacations training in Steinway's concert department and then joined the company full-time as a technician. In 1988 he left New York for the Falcone challenge. He says, "I wanted a situation where people were more committed to building high-quality pianos, as Steinway was a hundred years ago." Peter Mohr has now started his own restoration company, along with several of the Falcone/Mason & Hamlin builders. Peter Mohr agrees with Sara Faust in his preference for the vintage Steinways, but he believes the piano's design is so "inherently perfect" that every Steinway has the potential to be great.

And Santi Falcone? Who came from Sicily when he was fourteen and learned the piano business so well that he could make one? He lives in Carlisle, Massachusetts, a small town. He and his wife make chocolate candy now—Dante Confections—truffles and turtles. At home he plays a piano that he built, that has his name on it. "Yes, that's very satisfying. And it's a very beautiful piano, made of rosewood."

In the June weather, inside an air-conditioned room with the shades drawn against the early sun, my piano begins to settle down. We can keep the temperature at seventy-four, and the humidity stays close to that figure. Thunderstorms continue to roll through in the evenings. I come up out of the subway into a yellow light with towering dusty clouds moving on east. There are tree branches, cracked by lightning, lying across the wet streets. I join the men in the neighborhood, standing with briefcases, holding summer jackets, talking about a downed pear tree and someone's flooded basement. When I was a kid in Kentucky, living three blocks away from the downtown business section, the businessmen would be walking home in the late afternoon, ending their days at five o'clock. They'd sit on the front porch and read the evening newspaper, waiting for dinner. I thought that's the way it would be when I grew up, but now it takes me an hour to get home and it's past eight o'clock.

I go on in the house to make a martini, with a glass from the freezer, and a sliver of lemon rind. I play

"Santa Lucia" on the Miracle keyboard, then move to the piano. It's an Italian folk song I first heard in Sweden, in Stockholm, during the week of the Nobel Prize awards, sung by young girls to bring light to December. I play it offhandedly, as if not especially caring about the next note, and it sounds like the beginning of a foreign film with the camera approaching the window of a crumbling villa in a shaded courtyard.

My piano—the Steinway 1098 upright—has Italy in its heritage by birthright and northern Germany by inspiration. Heinrich Englehard Steinweg became a cabinetmaker in the village of Seesen. He'd been an apprentice to an organ maker. And he started making pianos. But not many. D. W. Fostle, in his book *The Steinway Saga,* deconstructs much of the company's mythic history and writes of this time:

> *That some small number of pianos did emerge from the shop in the Steinweg homestead is certain; beginning when or how many in total will never be known. Who might have bought these instruments in the surrounding hamlets that were connected to Seesen only by the most primitive dirt trails cannot be divined. If a living were made from them alone, it was modest. A more likely scenario is that Heinrich Steinweg built the occasional piano, tuned and repaired any he could find, sold and fixed secondhand instruments of all kinds, and kept a large vegetable garden and livestock out of necessity.*

And from this beginning rose an American piano company. Fostle concludes his first chapter: "Although the *instrumentenmacher* Steinweg was born in Germany, his fame, after nearly a lifetime of incubation, was hatched in the New World. The Steinweg story is a story of America."

Would he have seemed special if you'd met him in lower Manhattan just after the family arrived in 1850? Hard to know. But surely he was old for this sort of thing. Heinrich Steinweg was fifty-three. He spoke no English; he couldn't *write* German. He had sold his home and his workshop in Seesen, and with the proceeds—about $780—the family sailed from Hamburg to New York. On the ship's record he listed his occupation as "farmer." But he quickly found work making soundboards for a piano manufacturer. His salary was $6 a week. His three older sons, Charles, Henry Jr., and William, also found jobs in the industry. They began making their own instruments in their spare time, in their house on Hester Street. And nine years later the Steinways (the name was Anglicized) were making more than one thousand pianos a year. As Fostle writes, "By any reasonable standard, the Steinways had become very wealthy very quickly." I've seen a Mathew Brady photograph of Heinrich Steinway, taken about this time. He looks impatient, wearing a frock coat and black hat, holding a walking stick. My guess is he was impetuous and brilliant, but also a tough worker and parent.

The Steinway men spent only a few years each as

craftsmen, leaving the factory bench to become managers, to help with sales and with research. They perfected the existing idea of an iron frame—the plate—to withstand higher string tensions. They borrowed the concept of overstringing; the bass strings can be longer since they lie over the treble strings, at a different angle. And they built some of the first eighty-eight-note pianos. Keyboards had been expanding for some time, but this would be the practical limit. D. W. Fostle explains that the eighty-eight notes encompass the tonal range of a symphony orchestra; also, pianists would have trouble reaching any extra notes, and trouble discerning frequencies that were much lower or higher.

Fostle also has a theory that the "modern" Steinway pianos, beginning by 1865, owe their distinctive and powerful tone to the fact that the Steinways, father and sons, all had hearing problems. Heinrich and Henry Jr. had become increasingly deaf, their affliction aggravated by the noise of piano making, by alcohol, and by their fondness for target shooting. It's quite possible, Fostle believes, that they were simply trying to design and build pianos that they could *hear.*

I start talking with other people, pianists, about instruments they've loved. The stories are reverential; ask about a favorite piano, someone's eyes will shine. George Todd, who teaches music at Middlebury College in Vermont, describes what he feels was an "epiphany." He and his wife, Megan, were in Italy, in Verona, and they went into a store to ask about a piano bench for

Megan's mother. George saw an interesting piano and sat down to play: "It was a Grotrian Steinweg, a German piano.* Not all that big, about the size of a Steinway B, maybe six foot eight. They let me play it for half an hour. I thought for a moment I was in heaven. It's almost a chemical thing. This piano was lyrical; it just had an extremely musical sound. It was effortless to get this singing quality. The connection between what I was hearing in my inner ear and what I was playing was unimpeded. I played some of the *Goldberg Variations.* I've been working on them for thirty years. I can play about twenty-four of them; there may be a couple that I'll never play. This instrument made it seem as if it were in reach. When we left, I said to Megan, 'Let's see if we can win the lottery so I can get that piano.' "

These are lovely stories to hear; most of us, though, will be happy to play just anything we can afford or find. As a young boy in Arkansas Scott Joplin played the pianos in the homes where his mother did domestic work; she'd do the cleaning and ironing, and he would practice the music he'd heard in church. The Russian virtuoso Anton Rubinstein said, "The piano is a lovely instrument. You must fall in love with it, with its sound, and then be tender with it to make it, in turn, be

* Wilhelm Grotrian was a partner of a Steinway son, Theodore, who built pianos for a time in Germany after his family had emigrated to America.

sweeter to you. Herein," he said as he laid his hand on the piano, "lies divine beauty." I take note that Rubinstein said *the* piano, not *this* piano.

It's a busy month. The pages of the June calendar are getting blurry. I'm distracted by the steamy weather and discouraged by the stories coming daily from Rwanda, about the massacres and troubles in the refugee camps. I work on a feature about the Actors Theatre of Louisville and spend several days talking with ministers and parents and youngsters for a report on prayer in the schools. I interview a lesbian couple and older gay men about the twenty-fifth anniversary of the Stonewall Riots in Greenwich Village. And right in the middle of all of it I *forget* about David Sudnow's piano seminar. I've lost the confirmation letter from Sudnow, with the date and times and location. I have vague pencil markings on several calendars and cryptic notes on pieces of paper I can no longer find. It's coming up this weekend? And this is Thursday afternoon? Don't worry, I'll pin it down tomorrow, but then Friday's a rush at *ATC* and in between interviews and writing chores I make frantic calls to New York. Manhattan information has a number for the Sudnow Method! But no, the woman there is only selling the Sudnow instructional videos and audiotapes. She doesn't know where the seminar is, or when, or how to get in touch with Mr. Sudnow. She could take a message? I remember the seminar's to be held at a piano store and start calling some of those, but everyone's busy, and no one's heard of David Sudnow. I recall he has an office in Princeton, New Jersey, but he's unlisted there. I try the 800 number information line—no luck. I call friends in New York—help! I go home and tear through messy piles of notes and newspaper clippings and old letters and receipts. Phone calls come back; no one knows. Early Saturday morning I decide against just flying to New York and taking the chance I can find the seminar.

And I spend the weekend angry with myself. How can I learn music if I can't even get to where I'm supposed to be going? I'm not even bothering to apply professional skills to the process; I've never forgotten an interview appointment and rarely been late; I've chased after a lot of planes and missed only one. Monday morning David Sudnow calls me at NPR. He's apologetic as if somehow it were *his* fault. "Don't worry," he says, "we'll get you in another one. And in the meantime I'm going to send you some stuff." (The seminar had been at a store in Manhattan called Piano/Piano. I should have figured.)

JULY

Throwing a firefly to Kansas could be easier than learning "Misty"

IN THE DARK THE CICADAS START. THEY ARE EVENING VIOLAS and celli, playing from ancient remembered scores. I've been reading Norman Mailer's *Of a Fire on the Moon* and a new book by Andrew Chaikin called *A Man on the Moon*, both about the astronauts and the Apollo missions. The twenty-fifth anniversary of the moon landing is coming up, and I'm trying to put a radio story together. I sit out in the backyard, with Will and the cicadas and fireflies, and watch the moon come up strong over the trees. Once, I remember, I was awakened by a moonrise. We were camped at the bottom of the Grand Canyon, sleeping close by the Colorado River. On past midnight the full blue-and-white phosphorescent moon slid across the narrow top of the canyon, spilling enough light to the bottom to read by.

Tonight's moon has a reddish gold city tint to it, but it's still quite a wondrous sight, especially if you're trying to imagine a makeshift landing craft, two men aboard, settling down on the dusty lunar surface. And I say out loud, "I could no sooner go to the moon than I could throw a lightning bug to Kansas." Then I go inside to write that down. It's a sentence I could use for my Apollo story, and I know that if I rely on memory tomorrow in the office, I'll miss a word or two and certainly the rhythm of the sentence.

This firefly image could also be used to describe the way I sometimes feel about the piano: that there's no chance I'll learn. But the analogy, however fanciful, is inaccurate. I *could* go to the moon; many people have. And I can certainly become a piano player.

When the lessons aren't going well, it helps to recall the story of the man who played piano *backward*. It's told in the book *In the Mind's Eye*, by Thomas West. A man named Delos Smith, despite dyslexia, graduated from college and found work as an economist. He had a great love of music and, as an adult, continued to take piano and singing lessons—even though his teachers told him he lacked any natural talent. But when he began studying harmony and counterpoint, his world changed. Smith had a "mirrored mind." As a child he wrote backward and often spoke backward. Those traits were overcome through training, but his musical sense was left unaffected. Then he studied the Bach *Inventions*, analyzed Bach's use of reverse order. Looking at the retrograde variations, he realized that despite his normal speech and writing skills, he still saw things in mirrored images. And then one night, when he was tired and trying to practice at the piano, he started playing the music backward: "I played song after song. I played Bach. I played Mozart. I felt no fatigue. I was on an adrenaline high. Euphoria had a new meaning. Of course, I played everything backward, but I was really playing it."

In the movie *Little Man Tate*, which is about a seven-year-old prodigy, there's a different sort of backward piano story. Fred Tate is so bored by the music lessons in school that he plays the songs backward when it's his turn at the keyboard. (His mom, a cocktail waitress, played by Jodie Foster, has to sell the piano in their apartment: "Money's been tight." She *paints* a replacement piano on the wall. Fred says, "You didn't paint the right number of notes.")

The lights are on in the house next door, and I think of my neighbor Jean. She's a dance critic, has been for decades (she saw Nureyev with the Kirov Ballet in Moscow the evening before he left for the West, to defect). A year ago Jean decided she wanted to try to write and produce dance stories for radio; most of her experience had been in print. Neenah and I were encouraging, but I thought, *Gee, it's late in her career to be taking on an entirely new art form; I've been doing this for twenty years, and it's hard.* But she bought a tape recorder and learned fast and sounds great and already has had several long dance features on NPR's *Morning Edition.* I watched her one day in an edit booth, cutting and splicing audiotape. The work was going slowly, but she was smiling. Just another skill. Jean already is a super pianist; it is her music that we hear through the open windows on summer evenings. And there's pride in her eyes when she asks me how my piano playing is going.

I go in the house and turn on the Miracle program and start working through the familiar phrases of the "Blue Danube." A satisfaction, an ease, of beginning to play the piano as an adult is that we already know these songs; we can sing the melodies, and we've danced in waltz time.

That familiarity turns out to be a big part of the operating philosophy of the Sudnow Method. Four cassette tapes arrive, and a small wire-bound book with Sudnow's picture on the back. He has dark hair down over his forehead, hands with very long fingers. The tapes are called "The Weekend Seminar." This is what I missed in New York; only these tapes are from sessions in Phoenix, 1994, and Chicago, 1988. The sound is the same: a meeting room in a hotel, a piano, a microphone for Sudnow, a group of hopeful players—some beginners, some with many years' experience, most with a year or two of childhood lessons.

Tape 1, Side A begins with piano music. A jazz-tinged arrangement of "Here's That Rainy Day," which slides into "Ain't Misbehavin'." Then David Sudnow stops playing and asks, "How many of you have pianos sitting around the house with doilies and pictures of servicemen on them? Piano playing is the most failed-at social skill in the United States. There are eleven million unused pianos."

Sudnow is laughing along with his seminar group, but you can hear that he's serious. He thinks it's all been wrong, the way we've been taught: "For most people, piano lessons were unpleasant experiences—sitting next to a stranger." He plays chords as he talks, and little single-note runs along the keyboard. It's Sudnow's goal to be unnecessary by the end of the seminar on Sunday. He doesn't think that teaching should be done in "pharmaceutical doses," administered over a long period of time. "One of the reasons it's so hard to learn the piano is that it takes so long," he says. And he promises a breakthrough—"a wonderful, luscious, transcendent experience"—after about twelve weeks at the keyboard if you practice an hour a day and do it exactly the way he says. He doesn't believe in exercises; why bother practicing fifths up and down the keyboard for twenty minutes when you could be playing the fifths in songs? "Go for the tunes," he says.

It's easy to understand what David Sudnow has in mind. You could learn this stuff and go play cocktail piano in the Holiday Inn or work at a piano bar. If you can figure out the *melody* of a song, you can add some chords and you've got it; you're playing by ear. I remember reading an obituary for Henry Mancini, who died recently. It said he wrote "Moon River" on the white keys, within a span of nine notes, so that Audrey Hepburn would have an easy time singing it in *Breakfast at Tiffany's*. I went straight to the piano and found that melody in just a couple of minutes. If I had known a couple of chords and when to play them, I'd have the whole song. Sudnow says these songs, from movies and Broadway shows, are really *folk* songs and that we, as folk, ought to be playing them. "Let's turn the piano into a folk instrument and let the adults learn the kind of music they can enjoy. Teach the adults, not the seven-year-olds; the seven-year-olds ought to be learning to read and write."

The melody of a song, he says, is easy to find. "It's not like looking for the fuse box in a darkened base-ment." The melody is laid out along the path of a scale and as such lies close to the fingers of your right hand. Most of the songs we know have melodies that reside in the notes of the major scales. Each scale has only eight notes: "Your hand falls right into the melody."

I like the fact that Sudnow has reduced the expanse of the piano to, theoretically, a small batch of white and five black keys right there in the middle. But I guess I'd been looking for a secret way into the techniques of playing by ear, some sort of metaphysical approach. He's talking about some *work* here. Learn all the major scales. You start with C major—that's middle C and then the next seven white notes, stopping at the C an octave above. Then the first black key, B-flat, moving in steps up the octave. This continues with ten more beginning notes.

The Sudnow Method says memorize very few things, but memorize this: a whole, a whole, a half, a whole, a whole, a whole, a whole, a half. Or as he says it fast: awholeawholeahalf—awholeawholeawholeawhole—ahalf. That's how the notes *step up* along each scale path. A step *from* a white key *over* a black key *to* the next white key is a whole step. A step from the white key to the next black key is a half step, and from a white key to the next white key *without* crossing a black key is also a half step. You play back down the scale by reversing your fingersteps.

I try a test. Play a note a random, let that determine the scale. Let's see if I can find a song. The note I've hit is a G, so I'll use G major scale. I play the G with my thumb and think of *Some,* then the G an octave up for *where,* then the F-sharp (the only black key in the scale) for *o* and D for *ver* and E, F sharp again, and G—*the rainbow.* This just happens to be a melody that starts on the first note of the scale, and that note suggested the song. Seems pretty easy.

Mr. Sudnow turns stern. You must learn these scales. You must learn how they look visually because in the future the keyboard is going to be your sheet music. Here's how you practice. With the index finger of your right hand play each note of the C major scale, up and back down. Then the B-flat major scale up and down.

Continue for all twelve. Your goal is to be able to play all the scales within two and a half minutes; that's not very fast. Then play each scale up and back with the whole hand. Again, the elapsed time should be two and a half minutes. "And, folks," Sudnow warns, "don't make mistakes when you practice. Keep a good beat. Don't worry about a metronome; if you can walk in this room, your body has perfect time."

I try to practice the scales and find I can't play them in *any* time. It's hard to work out the steps up the keys, finding the whole and the half steps and then trying to remember the way back down. After about thirty-five minutes it all begins to sound inane and my index finger's getting sore from the plunking. The next morning there's a fresh start—with the door to the bedroom carefully closed—and I do only slightly better. Thirty-five more minutes after work, and on and on into July, trying to play all the scales perfectly. Once I almost make it but then feel like slamming my fist down on the keys when I mess up. At the same time, though, I'm practicing each scale with the whole hand; that seems much easier, but I'm still a mistake or two short of perfect.

We take a Saturday morning drive, with Will, out into Virginia, to a place in the foothills of the Blue Ridge called Graves' Mountain Lodge. We've been coming here for about ten years now; we found it one day when we were just wandering around this part of Virginia in my favorite old car, a 1966 faded-blue Plymouth Valiant (with a bench seat). We brought Will out when he was a puppy, and he would run in fast circles around the fields.

One Fourth of July we were here for fireworks. The people at the lodge invite everyone from the county, and the pickup trucks pull in early for suppertime picnics and a good view. We sat on a quilt in the middle of a crowd on a hillside. I'd brought a tape recorder; the explosions and the piercing whistles were echoing off the mountain ridges. And the next Fourth of July I used the tape for a sound essay about neighbors celebrating the holiday in the country and the pleasure of seeing fireworks close up, instead of being a half-mile away amid half a million people in Washington at the National Mall. On the tape you could hear excited kids with soft rural accents and mothers talking to their younger children. And the "whoomph" of the rockets soaring off and the deep reverberations from the valley. And Will, with young-sounding barks, half afraid, half adventurous. The Plymouth Valiant was stolen long ago. Will is now eight years old with a bad knee; the vet is talking about surgery. And our Fourth of July fireworks extravaganza this year consisted of a few bought-by-the-roadside sparkling, showering flares, set off in the backyard.

At lunch today at Graves' we have stewed tomatoes and shredded pork, and applesauce, beets. Blueberry cobbler. A great cup of coffee. And we look out at the mountains and decide to go up White Oak Canyon. The trailhead is a short drive away. Lots of city cars in the parking lot, lots of city people on the trail. A black Lab puppy is being carried back down, dripping wet. There's a creek that comes down the canyon. "He fell in." This is a hike we've made often. We like to do it fast. I remember being worried the first time Neenah and I came up this trail; I was just managing to quit smoking and was so far out of shape I was worried about my heart. I didn't tell Neenah. And in the years since, having started running, I've been amused at the thought that a four-mile uphill hike could be too strenuous. Will does pretty well today too. When he's stiff, you can hear a pop in his knee as the cartilage shifts. It sounds painful, and it may be. But now he's warmed up and the pop goes away and the trail's easy for him; he even barks belligerently at two backpackers. People with packs on look like Martians to dogs. Will does not choose, though, to jump in the pool formed in the limestone rock by a waterfall, two miles up in White Oak Canyon. We've been in this pool before; it's icy even in July, the water spilling down from the crest of the Blue Ridge, a few more miles up. Kids are yelling, sliding down the rock. And there's a chocolate Lab puppy, maybe twelve weeks old, splashing with them.

On the way back home Will sleeps, snoring at times, on a blanket on the backseat of the car. Neenah's napping, her head on a pillow against the window. And I'm driving along lost in piano thoughts. I feel as if I'm stuck right here in the middle of my first year of learning, playing the scales with one finger, over and over, trying to hit the two-and-a-half-minute mark. I can play some of the songs in the Miracle computer course, but the arrangements are starting to sound childish and unsatisfying. This first year could be the hard part, though. And maybe it could be the only hard part; somehow it has to get past being work.

There is much hope to be gained from a small book, published more than fifty years ago, called *Playing the Piano for Pleasure*. This book, which is still in print but hard to find, is pure enthusiasm; if you get *close* to it in a library or a bookstore, it will almost bounce off the shelf into your hands. The author is Charles Cooke, at that time a staff writer for the *New Yorker*. He says in his preface: "Playing the piano is my greatest joy, next to my wife; it is my most absorbing interest, next to my work. Therefore I believe I can safely hold that it stands, in relation to my life as a whole, just where a beloved hobby should stand."

Mr. Cooke says he intended his book to be inspirational. He writes:

I am thirty-six. Twenty-six of these years have been brightened and enriched by music. I was ten years old when, in my home in Cooperstown, N.Y., I first began to listen intently to my sister, Lucy E. Cooke, who, then as now, played the piano beautifully. For example, her playing of Beethoven's Pathétique Sonata *invariably put me in an emotional mist. To be able to play that sonata seemed to me one of the most worthwhile and glamorous achievements a human being could aspire to—a view I still hold.*

As a reporter for the *New Yorker*'s "Talk of the Town" section Charles Cooke—who often wrote as the magazine's Mr. Stanley, exploring obscure places in the city "and streets with names like Fteley Avenue and Yznaga Place"—had the chance to meet and interview the pianists Josef Hofmann, Artur Schnabel, Vladimir Horowitz ("Horowitz likes to drive his Rolls-Royce at a terrific clip"). "But here," he writes, "I make you privy to a secret my *New Yorker* editors don't know—I also invariably grill pianists for pointers which, though useless for the resultant untechnical story, are highly useful to me for *my* hobby. And therefore useful to every reader of this book, for I have taken pains to include every one of these pointers." (I must in fairness reveal the same sort of duplicity with regard to my *All Things Considered* editors, although in my case it has more to do with the desire to interview the pianists in the first place; I don't really *know* enough to be asking highly technical questions.)

So Charles Cooke has an interesting, steady job. A rebuilt "beloved" Steinway B (thirty dollars a month on the installment plan), a reawakened interest in the piano (he'd found a good teacher), and *one hour a day to practice* (he liked using a half hourglass to time the session). He says a "never omitted" hour each day will work wonders. "Five years ago, I looked at the music of Chopin's B-minor Scherzo and was dismayed. I was convinced that it was hopelessly and forever beyond me. I kept on working. Today I play it." He learned other Chopin works and the Brahms Rhapsody in G Minor, Debussy's "Clair de Lune," "Spanish Dance" by Navarro, "The Prophet Bird" by Schumann. At the end of the five years he had finished *memorizing* twenty-five compositions—had them firmly in his repertoire—and was working on a new list of twenty-five. All this accomplished in one hour a day. And Cooke says, "It is beside the point that I was born with little natural talent for the piano, and that my memory is a weak one which has to be bolstered with every memory aid I have been able to borrow or devise; we are talking about work here . . . tiring work, refreshing work."

The key to learning a difficult piece, for Cooke, is immediately to confront the "fractures." He uses the analogy of a broken arm or leg's becoming stronger at the point of the healed break. Cooke is intense about this:

I am now looking you straight in the eye and I am speaking slowly and rather loudly: I believe in marking off, in every piece we study, all passages that we find especially difficult, and then practicing these passages patiently, concentratedly, intelligently, relentlessly —until we have battered them down, knocked them out, surmounted them, dominated them, conquered them—until we have transformed them, thoroughly and permanently, from the weakest into the strongest passages in the piece.

It was a young Austrian pianist, Poldi Mildner, who taught all this to Cooke. They talked after her Town Hall debut in 1932. He wanted to know how she practiced Balakirev's "tremendously difficult" *Islamey*. She said, "I learn first the hard parts, *ja?*"

Mr. Cooke's book, read from my level, can seem at times esoteric—his lofty music examples and discussions of technique and theories about sight reading—but I get easily caught up in his enthusiasm, and I'm pleased by his rationale for the hard work: "Every music composition we collect becomes our friend—while we are thinking about learning it, while we are learning it, and transcendently after it is learned. It differs from every other composition as humans differ from each other. Like our human friends, it is a warmth in our heart."

Charles Cooke, in this 1941 book, states his personal goal as an amateur pianist: 125 pieces, memorized and retained. Five groups of twenty-five. He died in October 1977, and I'll bet he made it.

I'd be happy at the moment just to play a couple of songs. I stopped by a music store, shopped in the EASY PIANO section, and brought home "Bridge over Troubled Water" and a collection titled *The Best of Patsy Cline*, including "Crazy," by Willie Nelson. (Nelson wrote "Crazy" when he was a fifty-dollar-a-week songwriter in

Nashville; he still earns royalties from the song.) You play a slow opening statement, then the two really great notes: an A and a drop to the C. "Cra . . . zy." Those notes alone are worth the $10.95 price of the book, but you also get to learn "Faded Love," "Sweet Dreams," and, if you insist, "Three Cigarettes in an Ash Tray."

I also can do pretty well with the first page of the Paul Simon song; it's a satisfying arrangement. But I realize I'm finding excuses to stay away from practicing the scales. (David Sudnow, standing behind my piano bench, would say; "You're wasting your time and your money. Stick with my course, and you can play those songs by ear.") So I'm back to the one-finger drill, up and back down the twelve major scales. I'm happy to notice that when I play a wrong note, it truly does sound wrong, although I don't understand why. I've asked musician friends about this: How can you hear a wrong note, for example, in a song that you don't even know? The answers run from a discourse on harmonic physics to "Well, you've been listening to Western music all your life, and that's been a learning process."

David Sudnow also does not approve of the chord structure used in most sheet music that you'll pick up in the stores, and his courses teach you to play better ones. Don't play the clunky standard chords, he says. Take one of the notes out of the standard left-hand chord and play it up in the right hand. The left hand will play two-note chords, and there's lots of action in the right, with the song's melody staying on top, played by the

little finger. He explains this open-chord voicing technique at length on his tapes and demonstrates the differ-
ences at the keyboard, but he wants me to see and feel
the difference in *my hands*. He wants me to learn
"Misty." He plays it through once; it's quite a sophisticated version. If you walked into a bar and the waiter
brought your drink and the pianist started up with this
tinkly jazz arrangement (maybe someone has said, "Play
'Misty' for me"), it would sound just right. And I don't
have to learn any music. There's a booklet that comes
with the Sudnow Method tapes, with note diagrams for
"Misty." Small drawings of the keyboard, showing the
location of middle C, and then dots to indicate the
opening chords of "Misty." Black dots on the white
keys that are to be played, and white dots on the black
ones. Notes that are struck individually are indicated by
name. So you would play three two-handed chords—
"Look at me"—then a single note, another single note,
then two more chords, and you're ready for "as a kitten
up a tree."

Sudnow wants you to have confidence in this song,
play it with style right from the beginning. Sure, those
three opening chords can be tough to get into your
hands, but they *sound* great. Play that first right-hand
chord over and over; lay your hand in your lap and pick
it up quickly and play those notes. Get those chords
down and go on to "I'm as helpless—" I work for
ninety minutes, and it seems to feel possible. The big
challenge in this system comes right at the start:

"Misty" could take ten weeks for a beginner to learn. The next song, using the same dot notation, might be learned in six weeks, the third one three weeks. Soon you start figuring out the chords yourself, and new songs require two weeks' work. After that you're playing by ear, and David Sudnow says, "I don't think there's anything you can do that can change your life as much."

In the mornings with coffee, in the evenings after dinner, I play the opening of "Misty." A week goes by. I'm figuring out the dots and trying to memorize as I go along. Sudnow says, "Here's how you memorize this. Learn the first page and tear it off and burn it. Then do the same with the second page." I don't quite trust him on this point. By the time the second Sunday night comes around I'm playing the song past the second page. Neenah's listening as she's taking a bath before bedtime, and she comes out with a happy tear in her eye; she loves the chords in the phrase "You can say that you're leading me on—"

Well, you bet I can play the piano, I'm thinking. But at the same time I'm looking at nine more weeks of playing nothing but "Misty," and it's not even a song I like very much. "Oh, you'll hate 'Misty' and me for the first weeks," David Sudnow says on the tape, but he promises a phenomenal growth curve.

AUGUST

I'm riding this piano bicycle through the puddles, and there's a big wet streak up my back

TAKE A HOT MORNING, LATER ON IN SUMMER. MAKE IT A Sunday. Let the newspapers wait out on the front lawn. Let your wife sleep, whisper to the dogs. Bring a mug of coffee into a chilled room. Put Keith Jarrett's *The Köln Concert* CD in the player. Turn it up a touch loud for early morning. The solo notes start. A piano, a stage, an audience: all of it happening twenty years ago, but it sounds as if the pianist is simply—at this moment—imagining what he might play an instant before his fingers move to the keys.

The sun comes through the dusty, smudged window. The small birds, reds and flashing yellows, dart to the feeder by Neenah's flower bed. Jarrett plays bright cascades of notes high above a three-note pattern in the bass. A melody starts. The left hand grows stronger, insistent. There's a sudden resonant beat; somehow he's tapping on the piano. And the chords roll on. Jarrett seems surprised. "Oh!" you hear him say as he plays a lilting, repeating pattern. His voice is half picked up by the piano mike. It's as if he were a fan sitting in the first row, saying, "Wow, are you listening to this?" The music slows for a moment, returning to a simple bass pattern, then builds into the melody again, Jarrett's right hand moving up and down the keyboard, remembering blues and long nights in clubs playing jazz and afternoons wandering through classical themes.

Then the notes become hesitant, experimental. And the sun glows through the window. You think of the strange dreams in the night and the promises you've made for the day ahead: phone calls to return, a book that you have to read for an interview, the Sunday papers. Maybe there's time for a long bike ride. You could cook something nice. . . .

Keith Jarrett's solo in Cologne is over, surely. He's just playing a few tinkly chords. Maybe fifteen minutes have gone by. But then there's a stream of sparkling harplike notes and the left hand picks up the melody in chords like a church organ and the music moves faster and louder and Jarrett is almost orgasmic. "Yeah."

A final breath of the theme in single right-hand notes, and it's over. The applause comes only as an afterthought; it's just polite. The audience has been away with Keith Jarrett in more than twenty minutes of improvisation. They know it, he knows it.

Keith Jarrett is close to my age. He began piano study at age three. He started improvising at seven. I think I'll wash this window, looking into the backyard.

Another famous piano moment is one I've been hearing since perhaps *I* was seven. It's Jess Stacy's solo on "Sing, Sing, Sing," from the Benny Goodman 1938 Carnegie Hall concert. This was an unusual booking for the Goodman band, popular as it was in ballrooms and on radio. But on Sunday night, January 16, jazz fans were standing in the aisles and even sitting on the stage at Carnegie Hall as Benny Goodman walked out with his clarinet. "Don't Be That Way" was the first song; you can sense the audience is with the band from the first note. They've come to see Goodman, and Harry James playing trumpet. They're cheering right away for Gene Krupa's flashy drumming. Also *Teddy Wilson's* piano playing. Wilson was featured with the Benny Goodman Trio and Quartet numbers. Jess Stacy worked with the band and backed up the singers; he was rarely given a solo. Whitney Balliett, the *New Yorker* jazz writer, says that Stacy's solos, when they did come, would seem hurried: "The sparkling bell chords drifted away like smoke, the quiet, flashing runs disappeared almost before they registered, and the silken tone verged on transparency."

This was to be a different night, there in Carnegie Hall, near the end of an inspired concert, near the end of the band's showpiece number "Sing, Sing, Sing." Benny Goodman nodded at Jess Stacy. His turn. Whitney Balliett's description, in his book *American Musicians: Fifty-six Portraits in Jazz*, is the equal of the music:

> The solo lasted over two minutes, which was remarkable at a time when most solos were measured in seconds. One wonders how many people understood what they were hearing that night, for no one had ever played a solo like it. From the opening measures, it had an exalted, almost ecstatic quality, as if it were playing Stacy. It didn't, with its Debussy glints and ghosts, seem of its time and place. It was also revolutionary in that it was more of a cadenza than a series of improvised choruses. There were no divisions or seams, and it had a spiralling structure, an organic structure, in which each phrase evolved from its predecessor. Seesawing middle-register chords gave way to double-time runs, which gave way to dreaming rests, which gave way to singsong chords, which gave way to oblique runs. A climax would be reached only to recede before a still stronger one. Piling grace upon grace, the solo moved gradually but inexorably up the keyboard, at last ending in a superbly restrained cluster of upper-register single notes. There was an instant of stunned silence. . . .

Thirty-six years later Balliett had a chance to ask about that solo. Jess Stacy remembered it well:

> *Benny generally hogged the solo space, and why he let me go on that way I still don't know. But I've thought about it, and there are two things that might explain it. I think he liked what I'd been doing behind him during his solo, and I think he was mad at Teddy Wilson and Gene Krupa and Lionel Hampton, because they had all told him they were leaving to form their own bands. When I started to play, I figured, Good Lord, what with all the circus-band trumpet playing we've heard tonight and all the Krupa banging, I might as well change the mood and come on real quiet. So I took the A-minor chord "Sing, Sing, Sing" is built around and turned it this way and that. I'd been listening to Edward MacDowell and Debussy, and I think some of their things got in there, too. I didn't know what else to do, and I guess it worked out pretty well.*

Stacy left Benny Goodman later that year, played with Bob Crosby, tried starting his own band, and by the late forties had given it up and started playing in piano bars in California. Then he took a job working in the mailroom of Max Factor and left the piano alone until well into his retirement, when he was coaxed into playing a few dates and going back into the studio.

"Misty" is supposed to be my one and only song this month. I've set a goal to get it memorized before September. I'm trying to do it in six weeks instead of the ten that David Sudnow said might be necessary for a beginner. And I'm still playing the major scales, with a single finger, then with the whole hand; it's going to be awhile before I'm consistently perfect within the two-and-a-half-minute limit.

On the hot nights coming home from NPR, though, I'm discouraged thinking about the *work* of learning "Misty." I want to get something to eat, watch a little of the Orioles baseball game on television, sit down at the piano, and play whatever comes to my fingers. I find, easily, the melody to "Let Me Call You Sweetheart." We've been to a couple of Orioles games this summer, and if you drive up to Baltimore early enough, you can watch batting practice. I enjoy the kids; they have determined eyes and fielders' gloves and short haircuts. A bat cracks against the ball, and I'm seeing the ballpark in 1950s black-and-white. And then a small town on the Ohio River. Me and my twin brother. Crew-cut blond hair, baseball caps, goofy grins. And our grandfather taking us for a drive on Sunday afternoons in a big black Plymouth, and we would sing together: "When You and I Were Young, Maggie" and "The Old Rugged Cross." He'd smile and wave his cigar and sing, "Let me hear you whisper that you love me too." And if I play just three of those notes on the piano, I'm back in the kitchen, at the big yellow table, having supper. With my brother, my mom, my grandparents (my dad's away in the navy).

This summer I've been riding my bike to work, returning on the subway in the evening; you can take a bicycle on the Metro after 7:00 P.M. The trip in the morning runs about fifty minutes; it's mostly downhill, and I feel good after I get to NPR and take a shower in the men's locker room in the basement. But it can be a nasty commute. The drivers are aggressive, furious already in the mornings. The intersections have difficult, oblique angles. You get hit with blasts of hot exhaust, and you roll through the oily clouds of diesel fumes from the buses. I ride with the memory of two bike injuries in a year (the broken collarbone and earlier a sprained neck; both times I'd hit a hole), and surely another accident is coming. Yet I do this for exercise, and the bicycle makes the day move faster. I also do it to have some control. The subway makes me stare straight ahead, slows my walk to a trudge.

Among the newspaper clippings and phone messages and Post-It notes surrounding my desk at NPR, I find this quotation (it's been around so long I hardly notice it anymore): "I believed I could live on sunlight, subway noise, and smoke." I don't recall who said that, and it's certainly about the New York City subway rather than Washington's, but for a period in my life it was quite a romantic notion. I now have another quotation taped to the wall, a fragment of a poem by Tomas Tranströmer:

> After a black day, I play Haydn,
> and feel a little warmth in my hands.

The hot winds of August continue. Haiti's troubles get worse. There are forest fires in the Northwest. A baseball strike begins. The Woodstock twenty-fifth anniversary stories start showing up. I talk with the author of *Patsy: The Life and Times of Patsy Cline.* And with rock and roll guitarist Dave Alvin, formerly of the Blasters, about his boyhood days in Bakersfield, California, sneaking into the music clubs at night. In the hallway at NPR someone said, "Dave Alvin again? You've interviewed him before."

"No, couldn't be," I said, "I'd remember."

But the computer's memory defeated mine: "Dave Alvin, *ATC,* 1986."

And someone else, a younger colleague, said, "I remember that Dave Alvin interview. I loved it. He was my hero. It inspired me to try to get a job at NPR, and I've been here seven years now."

I found it quite discouraging that I'd forget. And it was a face-to-face interview too; he was playing here in Washington. I usually can remember talking to people whom I've actually met (sometimes, introducing myself over a satellite circuit to an interview guest in a distant city, I'll borrow a saying from back in Kentucky: "We've howdy'd but haven't shook"). Perhaps, though, after some twenty-five thousand interviews, the numbers are just catching up with me. It was nineteen years ago this month that I drove up to Washington with all my clothes, a few books, a good Advent radio, and an IBM Selectric typewriter to start working for *All Things Considered.* I was a production assistant. My salary was ninety-six hundred dollars (I'd been making sixty-five hundred dollars at the University of Kentucky radio station). I was planning to stay in Washington only a couple of years.

Seven days go by, and I realize I haven't touched the piano. On a Saturday night I close the door to the office and make some resolutions. Give Sudnow's ideas a chance, I tell myself; at least finish "Misty." And I write a two-hundred-dollar check to reserve a place at the Autumn Sonata, the piano camp for adults run by Erica vanderLinde Feidner's parents. I'd phoned to make sure there was room. "Of course," Rosamond, Erica's mom, said, "do come. But we're filling up fast." And yes, she said, we're expecting at least two other beginners; you'll have company. The total cost for the ten-day Sonata is $750, including a place to sleep and all your meals. You could spend as much on a plain old vacation, and this one's in Bennington, Vermont, right when the leaves are turning.

And I decide to put the Miracle keyboard away for now. It's exciting to play "Chariots of Fire," with a full synth accompaniment, but I ran into annoying trouble trying to learn "Happy Birthday." I could handle the melody okay, but my left hand just could not play the chords at anything approaching real music tempo. And I'm tired of the Miracle complaining about quarter notes and half notes, demanding that I play in the proper time.

That leaves "Misty." I sit at the piano until past eleven at night, then lie in a hot tub trying to relax my back muscles so I can get to sleep. I learn some new phrases, then go back and play as much of the song as I know. It's not lovely any longer. The chords sound stressed. Perhaps it's my still out-of-tune piano, or quite possibly it's my hearing, which seems to be overly sensitive.

How then, it might be helpful to wonder, does a *real* pianist do it? How does a concert artist get ready for two months of appearances, in several states? How do you memorize, how do you *perfect* several hours' worth of music, have them so firmly in your consciousness that fear and fatigue and bad lighting and slippery keys and a coughing audience won't shake the notes loose?

Edmund Battersby has curly black-gray hair, a black-and-white sweater, and black jeans. He sits on the piano bench, answering a beginner's questions. I took the train up from New York City to Tarrytown to meet him. His picture in my mind came from one of his CDs. In the liner notes for Granados's *Goyescas*, he's shown smiling, piano-side, with the assumed elegance of white tie and tails. My next-door neighbor Jean, the dance critic–pianist, said, "Why don't you go up and meet Eddy if you get a chance? You'd like him." She was right to expect that I'd be intimidated by a classical artist, but he turned out to be just a guy who teaches in the music department at Montclair State University and has a concert career the rest of the time. He's a Juilliard graduate and for several years has been a Steinway Artist, meaning that, in return for his endorsement, Steinway & Sons will try to have a concert grand available for his performances, anywhere they might be.

He is practicing today on a borrowed 1925 Model A that needs work. The paper-thin sheets of ivory are shedding off the keytops. "I love the touch of ivory," he says. "It's like what Willa Cather wrote in one of her novels about felt. She said it drank from the fingers. You can feel the ivory keys of a piano drink from your hands."

He's working in this room, at this piano, every day. Four to six hours every day, building the repertoire for his upcoming concert schedule.

"When you walk in here, how do you find the mood to practice?" I ask.

"I listen to operas, and string quartets. Listening to other music gets my ears going. I put on the tapes and walk around the room, do some stretches, massage my knuckles and fingers—my hands will usually be cold. And I'll look at some scores, just read them to wake up my brain. Then I sit down and play some two-voice pieces: Bach, Scarlatti; simple things. Then some Liszt and Chopin études. Some pianists don't return often enough to the *beginning* of their learning; they just go back to the last place that was *difficult*. Dancers, you know, always seem to be going back to take beginner classes, but musicians don't do it. And I'm a born-again scale practicer. I've come back to it, and it's helping. I play the scales in octaves, thirds, sixths and tenths to keep my interest up."

He plays some quick, spinning runs up the keyboard to show me how the piano sounds. Eddy Battersby has been performing for thirty years, since he was a teenager. Hundreds of concerts. Is there one special memory? His answer comes quickly, but he speaks slowly: "I was playing in the middle of winter in Blue Hill, Maine. Schubert. At the First Congregational Church in Blue Hill. It was a copy of the Graf piano. Conrad Graf made pianofortes in Vienna in the early 1800s—this is well before pianos had cast iron plates, and it's a more delicate, transparent sound. The piano I played was made by a builder in Maine. The church was full; there were three hundred fifty people there, and Blue Hill's a small town. I played the Schubert B-flat sonata and the last four Impromptus, and for me it was just a transcendent experience. There's something here you don't get in recordings. There's a great power in great music being effectively played, when people fall under its spell and are united in a common experience. Sometimes in a concert you get the feeling that everyone in the audience is *breathing* with you, but it's really even more intense than that, and time takes on a different dimension."

I ask for a favor. "Play something *big* for me. I'd like to stand right here by the keyboard and get a sense of what it sounds like when someone's really playing with power." His hands thunder down onto the keys and roll up the octaves, and a steely, glittering sound is ripped from the strings and bangs into the air while deep chords pound up from underneath. The notes infuse your body like electrons. The piano becomes small under his hands. The piano shakes.

Eddy Battersby laughs. "That's part of the cadenza from the Rachmaninoff First Concerto. I played it with the Pittsburgh Symphony."

Battersby is now forty-four years old. The hard work of preparation is not difficult for him. "Performing, you understand, is an obsession." As for his career, he believes the better years are ahead; he's looking forward to fifty. Vladimir Horowitz would have certainly agreed. And Arthur Rubinstein had said that his playing wasn't to his own satisfaction until he was close to eighty years old.

George Shearing was born in 1919. He moves confidently through the crowded tables at the King of France Tavern in Annapolis, Maryland. He's holding on to the arm of his bass player as they walk to the bandstand. Shearing has been blind since birth. He jokes about it: "I played with the George Shearing Quintet for twenty-nine years. Then I got bored. Closing my eyes during performances made no appreciable difference." And about the after-show sales of his latest CD: "I can assure you that all profits go directly to the blind." The laughter is only polite; these are jazz fans, Shearing fans.

The air smells of cool cigarette smoke. The young bass player has tinted glasses. Mr. Shearing is wearing a blue blazer and gray pants, dark glasses. He looks straight ahead and smiles and nods, and his hands move to the keyboard.

It is the light, almost tinkling sound with quiet chords from the albums we had when I was a teenager and should have been listening to rock and roll. My mother bought me a set of drummer's wire brushes, and I'd play along with the music, swirling the brushes around on the album covers, tapping the rim of a wastebasket. The special "Shearing sound" goes back to 1949. He was inspired by the saxophone section of Glenn Miller's band and developed a "locked hands" style. *The New Grove Dictionary of Jazz* says, "Each note of the melody is harmonized with a three-note chord in the right hand, the left hand doubling the melody an octave below. . . ." The *Dictionary* adds: "In Shearing's quintet the upper melody note was then doubled by the vibraphone, and the lower one by the guitar. . . ."

George Shearing moves through the old songs in pretty much the old way, the audience smiling, with quick riffles of applause when a favorite tune begins. He seems to take his pleasure from the bass player's solos, humming along and laughing. And then a drifting start to "My Romance." I don't think Neenah knows the song, but the images float in my mind as he plays: "My romance doesn't need a castle rising in Spain. . . ." His smile becomes soft and real. He's thinking of the lyrics too. He plays as if sensing with his hands the precise notes that *this night* would best go with the words. "My romance doesn't need a thing but you." At moments he looks surprised. Neenah takes my hand at the song's end; she has a quick shake of her head, as if to disbelieve the emotion.

And how about an eighty-one-year-old boogie-woogie piano player who can make you follow him off the bandstand and ask for the first-ever autograph of your life? It's a blues club, big dance floor, beer and baskets of french fries and burgers, and a pool table that doesn't stop for the music. Saturday night. Mr. Pinetop Perkins would play, the newspaper ad said. Pinetop Perkins— "Delta Bluesman"—whom I missed seeing in May down in Oxford, Mississippi. We arrive late, and he's later. There's time for a slow pitcher of beer and some songs by the band, and then Mr. Perkins is introduced, and someone helps him through the dark up to the piano bench. He's wearing a dusty black suit and a gray hat; his face and hands are Delta-creased. He grins to the crowd and then *whomps* the keyboard—it's a Roland electric—and plays the blues. These are the longest, oldest fingers I've ever seen play. And they would defy a young man's to follow. He rolls into a set, singing

"Chains of Love," and "Caldonia." The band's good, but I'd just like to sit up there close and watch the piano being played.

There's a boogie-woogie mystery here. We had a 78 rpm record when I was little called "Pine Top's Boogie Woogie." I remember its spinning around fast, a raspy, distant sound to the piano. When I was taking some lessons at twelve or so, I had some sheet music for the same song and loved trying to play it. Clarence Pine Top *Smith* wrote that music; it's said to be the first song that used the term *boogie woogie* in the title. Others had played the form before. In the late 1890s there was a fellow named William Turk; he weighed three hundred pounds and was hard to forget. Pianist Eubie Blake later described Turk's playing: "He had a left hand like God. He didn't even know what key he was playing in, but he played them all. He would play the ragtime stride bass, but it bothered him because his stomach got in the way of his arm, so he used a walking bass instead. I can remember when I was thirteen—this was 1896—how Turk would play one note with his right hand and at the same time four with his left. We called it sixteen; they call it boogie-woogie now."

When Clarence Smith, in his 1928 recording, sang (and talked) about "boogie woogie," he meant both the music and the dancing that would go on at a party. "Shake it, don't break it," he'd say. And he invited the girl "with the red dress on" to come over by the piano and dance. Jump ahead a few decades, and you have

Jerry Lee Lewis singing, "Shake it one time for me," and Ray Charles with "What'd I say": "See the girl with the red dress on, she can do the *Birdland* all night long."

And then *Willie* Perkins, in what sounds like a blues legend deal with the devil, came along to borrow Mr. Smith's song and his name. In 1951 Willie Perkins, recording for Sam Phillips's Sun label in Memphis, had such a hit with "Pine Top's Boogie Woogie" that *he* became identified with the song. Why fight it? Clarence Smith had died in 1928, shot by accident one night in a club. His nickname lives on strong with Pinetop Perkins. To hear Perkins sing, above the rumbling bass notes, is to *see* the late-night rent party in someone's apartment: smoky light and the smell of sweet wine.

And then late on a Friday night I find myself driving fast up Interstate 81 through the Shenandoah Valley in Virginia on the way home from an interview. It's been a hot, messy day, and I've turned off the air conditioner just to let some real air in through the windows. I'm over the speed limit, but the trucks come roaring up behind me, flashing lights. When it gets past eleven and I'm still out on the road someplace, I always start thinking about AM radio, about the great nights in the fifties and early sixties; you'd drive just for the music. AM radio is now just a vibrant memory; I can't seem to pick up the clear-channel fifty-thousand-watt stations anymore, and you can't tell me the new car audio systems sound better than the old Delco tube-type radios.

I do have a CD player in the car, and riding along close to midnight, I've been listening to Eric Clapton's blues album *From the Cradle.* It's technically stunning, live studio music with few overdubs, and I'm only a little put off by Clapton's new white Gap T-shirt and his pretend-ravaged blues voice, but I don't realize how little *satisfaction* the songs are bringing until I push "eject" and slip Pinetop Perkins's CD into the player. Just one guy at a piano and a microphone a couple of years ago at a studio in New York, the songs interspersed with interviews, Pinetop talking about the misadventurous old days. There's a grin in his singing, and his playing has an accomplished energy; if you've done this a thousand times in blues clubs, you can make that *next* chord sound like a surprise. And his notes rollick and float *around* the center of the beat; any second now *he'd* get up and start dancing.

I make the turn out of the valley at Front Royal and head east on I-66, seventy miles to Washington. I'm looking for a patch of dark forest off to the right of the highway. One night Neenah and I saw three million fireflies in those woods. There *are* a few tonight; there could never be as many as before. And I remember the hot Friday evening ten years ago, when we roared past this spot going the other way, driving into the mountains after a rough week at work; we'd left NPR at seven and in five minutes we were on the interstate, flying, listening to Bob Seger's pure rock and roll and drinking champagne from paper cups. It was a time when just a touch was exciting and the music matched it.

I'll be home in an hour, tired, wanting a bath and sleep. I realize I'm not especially looking forward to the weekend ahead, and the reason is "Misty." The piano *listening*'s been great, but *my* summertime learning curve has collapsed. I've come to dread the scale exercises. I can play "Misty" at a slow tempo, reading the dot diagrams, but I can't seem to memorize it. Three pages of the music stay in my mind; the final two will not. I've played "Misty" too much. The piano's out of tune. Who cares?

SEPTEMBER

An assignment in Ireland, two weeks off in Maine. What's a piano?

I HAD ALWAYS WANTED TO SEE BELFAST. AND THE TRIP CAME up quickly with the announcement of a cease-fire between the Protestant and Catholic paramilitaries. A producer said, "Someone should go, let's ask Noah."

"I'll call Neenah," I said. Our vacation was starting; she'd planned to drive to Maine, taking our dog Will. I was going to fly; I'd had a ticket for a month. But it would be Northern Ireland instead.

"Of course you should go," Neenah said. "What a chance."

I walk along the morning streets of Belfast admiring the young women on their way to work, with deep black hair and creamy-white blushed complexions. The people seem vibrant, friendly. "Belfast is the greatest wee town in the world," someone tells me. Yet the British troops are still on the streets, automatic weapons poised; the cease-fire may be only a hopeful pause. The army has built forts atop the apartment blocks. Far above in the sky, ominous and chattering, the dark helicopters hover, with their surveillance equipment. They can read license plates from there, can listen to conversations on the sidewalks or in the stands at a soccer game. Meanwhile, on the streets, people hope for a return to "decent crime"—just drugs and robberies. In the bookstores you'll find a violence section, histories and novels about the past quarter century in Northern Ireland. You can even buy a book called *An Index of Deaths*. The Protestants refer to this time as the Troubles; Catholics call it the Struggle.

The reporting work begins: A bomb goes off at the Sinn Féin office; I take a taxi, check the damage, find a phone, file a story. We rent a car and drive south to a country village on the border with the Republic of Ireland. The Irish Republican Army sympathizers are moving blocks of concrete into the river, creating an illegal crossing. The soldiers, with binoculars, are watching from the tree line, up on the hill. Back in the city I watch a scurry of young boys running up to the Protestant side of the peace line, laughing as they throw stones across the wall. The stones go both ways across the wall in Belfast. "The older guys build snowballs, and the kids throw them," says a Protestant cabbie, once a loyalist militiaman, who takes us to his favorite bakery. A woman tells me of a teenager killed in front of her house late one night. It was his birthday, he was dressed up, and he'd been to a disco. He was shot because he was dating a Protestant girl. I play a few notes on an organ in a small neighborhood church that's been a repeated target of bombing and arson and realize that the piano has become a faraway thing in my mind.

I work a week of long days and, after a breakfast of scones and tea, get back on the plane at Belfast airport. I fly from Belfast to London, London to Boston, Boston to Bangor, Maine, where Neenah waits at the airport, with Will in the station wagon. There's a chilly rain; it's good to be in the old warm white Volvo, heading for a small yellow house by Penobscot Bay, with three weeks ahead for sleep.

"There's a piano at the church in Brooksville you can play," a friend told me. She spends most of her summers in Maine, an idyllic time, missing only a piano, and this year she'd asked to borrow an hour's practice each week in the small Methodist church. "It's a good piano," she said. "I make a little donation in return." But the idea of practicing, or of taking a lesson, now seems burdensome. I probably should admit I won't be able to go much further with David Sudnow's play-by-ear methods. I don't feel like turning on the Miracle computer course again. It's hard to see the piano in my future at all. And I've had plans for this to be a *sailing* vacation.

It's about an hour's drive from Bangor down to the coast and along the narrow roads that follow the inlets of Penobscot Bay. Neenah's driving, telling me about her time in Maine so far and I'm drifting off to sleep, but then I hear: "Guess whose boat I went sailing in yesterday?" I can venture no idea. "Joel White's Shellback," she says. I'm wide-awake now but pretend not to be. This was her first time in a Shellback, and if she didn't like it, what would I do about the one Eric Dow's boatshop is building as a surprise? (I had phoned earlier in the summer, asking if a Shellback could be ready. A small sailboat; I've been thinking of it as Neenah's piano. This boat has a direct connection to E. B. White—the writer's home was here in Brooklin, Maine, and his son, Joel White, designed the Shellback dinghy and built the first one. It's a lovely craft; it sails, it rows, you can put it on top of the car. Please paint it white, I had asked, and don't call the house or send a letter.) "What a silly boat," Neenah *could* say. "It's much too small to bother with." What she *does* say is "I loved it. What a great little boat." And I go on to sleep as she tells me about calling our friend Jane at the WoodenBoat School and about their lunch and Jane's suggestion that they borrow Joel's boat at his Brooklin Boat Yard dock. Several people Neenah saw that day knew that she would soon be a Shellback owner, but no one let on, and she was distracted anyway by the chance to meet Joel White. He's in his fifties now and sounds, she said, much like his father. We have a copy of *Char-*

lotte's Web on compact disc—three hours of E. B. White's voice telling his story of Wilbur the pig and his befriending spider. And the sailing was great, in the original Shellback. She and Jane, with a good breeze, went out of Center Harbor in Brooklin into Eggemoggin Reach. Jane insisted that Neenah be at the tiller. It was her first Shellback sailing lesson.

We drowse through the weekend. Slow movements and long naps; the weather's gray and low-spirited. I take Will on an hour's walk through the woods and notice that he tires more easily than the year before. I'm feeling the same way, as if I'm paying for the past year and especially the last week; Neenah said I looked gray when she picked me up at the airport. Today my mind can't stay with thoughts, and I just want to stand on the back porch and look out across the open water and breathe the wet air.

A trip into town seems necessary, though, for the newspapers and groceries. Neenah at least has the energy to talk about making a blueberry pie with mangoes; the quarts of blueberries on the roadside tables are three dollars each; there's nobody around, just leave the money in the box. There's a farmer's market open in Blue Hill. It's perfect produce time: heavy, proud tomatoes and beans, lettuce, onions, sweet corn. You're lucky if you like zucchini; it's free this time of year.

The wind stays strong. At first light Monday morning I can hear it roaring in off the water as I get up to let Will out the kitchen door so he can pee. He's been lying on his blanket on the floor through the night, but when we come back in I lift him up on the bed so we all can have an extra hour's sleep. Neenah murmurs contentedly and rolls over closer. The wind scares me. When I think of sailing our new boat, it's not on a sunny morning but in stormy weather that closes in quickly with dark, gusty winds and the boat slams sideways and spills over and we're suddenly in the frigid waters of Penobscot Bay—in danger just a hundred yards from shore. This fear is not entirely rational, and it's one I should confront. Wouldn't be a bad idea to take our new boat out on a sunny day and turn it over, just for practice. The water's so cold that you'd want to stay with the boat if it capsized. The trick would be to right it somehow and get back in. Neenah sleeps on with no reason for fear; she doesn't even know we own a boat. But she still has been talking about Joel White's Shellback and wondering if someone might have a used one for sale. I think the surprise is safe (or she's a fantastic actor).

After breakfast we drive over to Brooklin. "Just to look around," I say, trying not to seem nervous. There's the Morning Moon Café, and the grocery store, the pretty white library, the cemetery where Katharine and E. B. White are buried—and Eric Dow's boat shop.

We pull into Mr. Dow's driveway. There's a boat on a trailer in the yard, with a FOR SALE sign. I say, "Let's see what this one is." It's a seventeen-foot skiff, not of much interest. I notice a new white boat, on sawhorses, behind a half-open door, and Neenah follows me inside.

The boat is gleaming white with dark green trim, about eleven feet long. There's a man in work clothes standing beside it, smiling as we say hello. Neenah asks, recognizing the design, "Is this a Shellback? It's beautiful."

"Sure is," the man says.

"Are you building it for someone?"

He looks quickly at me. "It's for a customer," he says, with caution.

"How much"—Neenah is moving fast here—"would it cost to build one for us?"

"Don't answer that." I jump in.

And the builder—Joe—says, "Are you Noah?"

And I turn to Neenah and say, "This is your boat."

Joe is grinning, I'm laughing, and Neenah's eyes are wide. She's taking big breaths. In a second she's crying.

On our way back to the house we stop to buy a bottle of champagne and some film for the camera and call a friend to help us celebrate the launching. It's a shallow beach at low tide. Stanley helps us lift the Shellback off the top of the car, and the three of us carry it to the edge of the water. The boat weighs only a hundred pounds, and it lifts easily if you balance it right.

The sunlight is warm; the bay is calm. Will wanders around halfway in the water, crunching mussels with his teeth. The boat smells of new paint, and we're careful not to scratch it. Neenah puts on her boots, and we lay the boat on the water. She gets in, takes the oars, a slight push, and she makes a graceful turn away from land. Neenah knows the name of this boat. I'd read that it's bad luck to launch a craft unnamed; she's picked one out but hasn't told us. Later we'll find someone to paint it on the stern.

A wooden sailboat, eleven feet, six inches long, moves in large circles on a calm inlet of Penobscot Bay. A boat imagined, sketched, then cut, joined, and sanded, built by one person for another. It seems very much *like* a piano. And the intention of the craft is the same: to build an instrument of wood that offers service, and knowledge, and escape. The act of sailing itself seems to relate to music—a voyage conducted by the wind, with slow, stately passages, then gusty allegros. Other adjectives also match: "calm," "stormy," "tempestuous." And Adele Marcus, a well-known Juilliard teacher, once said, about her student's debut performances, "It's one thing to launch a ship. It's another to make it sail."

Neenah's face is alight as she rows. This is clearly *her* sailboat. Stanley and I watch from shore, drinking the champagne. We take a few pictures, but it's not a scene we'll forget.

The next morning it's good weather for a real voyage. Neenah rigs the sail on the boat; it's made from red Dacron. We take along the oars just in case, and our life jackets, and push off. I sit in front, in the bow, watching for lobster buoys, Will watches from up on the back porch, where he's tied, and Neenah sits low in the stern, at the tiller. The Shellback seems to like the weight of two people; she feels confident in the water. The small waves smack against the resonant wood of the hull. Neenah lets the sail out a bit, and the boat jumps ahead. When the wind's right and the boat is balanced, it's as if the world spins for a second as we float and dance on top of it. I'm still holding on tight to the gunwales, especially when Neenah tacks, swinging the sail around to change directions; I don't know how far this boat can heel without capsizing. I've talked through this with a friend who once did turn over in a boat much like the Shellback. "Get a big Clorox bottle and cut out the end of it and tie it in tight; you'll need a good bailer," he said, running down the checklist. "She won't sink, but you have to get a lot of water out of the boat fast, and then you can go in over the back, over the transom." It probably would make sense for us to take this Shellback over to a pond nearby—where there's not much wind and the water's warmer—and turn it over a couple of times for practice. But then I seem to be the only one worried about this, perhaps because Neenah's a much stronger swimmer. I only learned about ten years ago; she taught me in the small pool in the apartment complex where we were living. I noticed in the newspaper here that the town of Stonington, a fishing community out at the end of Deer Isle, is trying to raise money to build a swimming pool. Most fishermen can't swim, and the town would like to change that.

This is the seventh September we've come to Maine, to the small community of Harborside. It is simply a post office and one paved road separating Penobscot Bay from the pastures and forests. We've made a lot of friends here, and most of them get together every Wednesday evening for a sauna and a potluck supper. They are people who work alone—a carpenter, a writer, a blacksmith, a dancer, a market gardener, a couple who train rescue dogs—so their time together is valued and intense. Neenah and I have often been invited to the Wednesday saunas, but we always show up only for supper. The saunas are, quite naturally, nude, and we've been too shy. This year we say, Who cares? And we arrive with a pan of scalloped potatoes and a couple of towels.

There is fragrant woodsmoke rising from the sauna's chimney. We undress and hang our clothes on pegs and open the door to the dry heat. Find a place on the highest bench, put the towel down, sit back and begin to melt. There are about twenty people inside, women, men, and a couple of children. The talk is of the week and the weather. Lots of kidding—the laughing makes it easier to pretend I'm quite used to sitting around with a bunch of naked people. There's an explosion of steam as a ladle of cold water is splashed on the stove. After about ten minutes I head outside to a rope swing, tied to a tree at the edge of the pond, and before I can think about it, I'm dropping into the dark water, gasping, my body heat evaporating to cold in the half minute it takes me to swim over and haul myself up on the grassy bank. And then quickly back inside. I find myself interested in my wife's body, slick and shining in the sauna's warm light. Ten more minutes, then some fresh air outside, then the heat again. Conversations grow more spirited, happier. It's the same sort of excited glow that comes with cocaine.

Soon everyone's in the kitchen for fresh corn and yellow cherry tomatoes and vegetable lasagna and our potatoes, plus hard cider, homemade, and Geary's ale from Portland, down the coast. And you sleep well on a night like this, as you try to figure out how you could move to Maine and find a way to make a living here.

We go to the Methodist Church in Brooksville on Sunday morning. Most of the congregation is older; the pastor is a woman from Bangor who one hour later serves another church, twenty miles away. I watch the organist closely to see how difficult the hymns might be. During one of the prayers I notice her eyes are open; she's looking at the next music she'll have to play. I couldn't blame her.

I grew up as a Methodist in Kentucky, and it's good to hear these familiar chords again. "We Are Climbing Jacob's Ladder," "There Is a Fountain Filled with Blood," and "Glory Be to the Father": "As it was in the beginning/is now, and ever shall be/world without end/ amen, amen." And the hymn that would often be played as an invitational, at the end of the service when people would come forward to rededicate their lives to Jesus: "Just as I Am, Without One Plea," with the refrain: "O Lamb of God, I come, I come." (This hymn has six slow verses, plenty of time to get down front if you were planning to.) And I realize, looking through the hymnal, that I've got a pretty good chance of playing these songs. Just a couple of sharps or flats, and the left-hand chords are usually only two notes. I'll have to find a hymnal at home. But not now. The piano my friend told me about—the one I could come to practice on—sits at the other side of the church, but I'm still not curious about it. I remember that I'm set to go to piano camp—the Autumn Sonata—next month in Vermont, but I'm not even looking forward to that.

I do want to *read* about piano playing, though, and I find the book I've been looking for in the Blue Hill Library. I had read Otto Friedrich's *Glenn Gould: A Life and Variations* several years ago, but after seeing the movie *Thirty-two Short Films About Glenn Gould*, I wanted to go through it again. And I've seen recently a Canadian Broadcasting Corporation documentary on Gould and listened to some of Gould's own radio documentary work for the CBC.

We could have met, I've been figuring. It was in 1982 that he died. He could have called late one night to talk; that's how he stayed in touch with his friends. He'd almost quit traveling after he stopped playing concerts, retreating to Toronto and the recording studio at age thirty-one. If he had lived a few more years, he surely would have been an Internet pioneer. It's clear he would have loved communicating by ghostly phosphors spinning through the night along the fiber-optic lines and the satellite links.

Glenn Gould was also a radio guy; he slept with it on

and dreamed about what he heard on the newscasts every hour. We could have talked about tape editing. It was a fundamental part of both his piano recording technique and his audio documentaries. When you edit audiotape, when you cut it with a single-edge razor blade and splice it back together in a new place, you are shifting reality; the words, the notes you have excised no longer exist. It is a very private world. You are the only one who knows what happened. The finished product is presented as real. The process is at once craft, art, metaphysics.

Gould called his CBC work contrapuntal radio, and it began by happenstance. He was working on a program called "The Idea of North," featuring Canadians talking about the northernmost reaches of their country, and he found himself with far too much tape. He'd recorded five people, separately. Why not, he thought, have them come together for the program? "The Idea of North" is an hourlong *drifting* through the subject, with voices fading in and out and overlapping and creating their own textures and space, plus music, and sound effects used as music; he refers to a train in his program as being "our basso continuo." The voices of course were music too (and you'll see pictures of Gould in the CBC studios, waving a pen, *conducting* the interplay of the tapes). He created a scene in the train's dining car, by using three of his characters, talking but obviously not listening. Gould believed you could pay attention to more than one voice. He writes:

It's perfectly true that in that dining-car scene not every word is going to be audible, but then by no means every syllable in the final fugue from Verdi's Falstaff *is, either, when it comes to that. Yet few opera composers have been deterred from utilizing trios, quartets, or quintets by the knowledge that only a portion of the words they set to music will be accessible to the listener—most composers being concerned primarily about the totality of the structure, the play of consonance and dissonance between the voices. . . .*
I do believe most of us are capable of a much more substantial information intake than we give ourselves credit for.

This thought is very similar to a story Gould told as part of a commencement address at the Toronto Conservatory. He was talking to future performers and composers and recalled something that happened in his early teens:

I happened to be practicing at the piano one day—I clearly recall, not that it matters, that it was a fugue by Mozart, K. 394, for those of you who play it too—and suddenly a vacuum cleaner started up just beside the instrument. Well, the result was that in the louder passages, this luminously diatonic music in which Mozart deliberately imitates the technique of Sebastian Bach became surrounded with a halo of vibrato, rather the effect that you might get if you sang in the bathtub with both ears full of water and shook your head from side to side all at once. And in the softer passages I couldn't hear any sound that I was making at all. I could feel, of course—I could sense the tactile relation with the keyboard, which is replete with its own kind of acoustical associations, and I could imagine what I was doing, but I couldn't actually hear it. But the strange thing was that all of it suddenly sounded better than it had without the vacuum cleaner, and those parts which I couldn't actually hear sounded best of all. Well, for years thereafter, and still today, if I am in a great hurry to acquire an imprint of some new score on my mind, I simulate the effect of the vacuum cleaner by placing some totally contrary noises as close to the instrument as I can. It doesn't matter what noise, really—TV Westerns, Beatles' records; anything loud will suffice—because what I managed to learn through the accidental coming together of Mozart and the vacuum cleaner was that the inner ear of the imagination is very much more powerful a stimulant than is any amount of outward observation.

It's a safe guess that the young women and men in the audience simply blinked and said, "Sure," when Mr. Gould explained this theory. He was allowing them a glimpse into his musical neighborhood. Only a few lived nearby. In his Gould biography Otto Friedrich mentions Arthur Rubinstein, who "once took the score of an unknown piano concerto aboard a plane to Spain and then performed it from memory, and without any rehearsal." Friedrich says that Alicia de Larrocha has the same sort of ability. "These are no ordinary gifts, of course," he writes, "but neither are they unimaginable. Gould's gift virtually was." He could sight-read anything "at speed," as pianists say, meaning he could play the piece at the proper tempo the first time through. And he could apparently *memorize* at a glance. Otto Friedrich quotes a CBC producer who was challenged by Gould to name a piece of music that he thought Gould might not be able to play from memory. The producer "asked for specific sections of Strauss's *Burleske*, Prokofiev's Seventh Sonata, Beethoven's op. 31, no. 3, "as well as other works, all of which he could do instantly." Gould once said, "When I was in the womb my mother played the piano continuously." And throughout his life Gould kept trying to find a piano that played and sounded like the old Chickering that had been in his parents' lakeshore cottage.

Glenn Gould died—killed by a stroke—two days after his fiftieth birthday. And he was an old man. Stooped, withdrawn, gray. He'd long had high blood pressure and chest pains and severe colds plus scores of imagined ills. He depended on tranquilizers, and in later years it's likely he was addicted to Valium. Too many doctors, too much medication, no exercise, bad food. In his will his estate was split between the Humane Society in Toronto and the Salvation Army.

He had made more than eighty recordings in his career. One of them—Bach's Prelude and Fugue in C Major from *The Well-Tempered Clavier*—was included on a copper disk aboard the Voyager spacecraft, two explorers launched for the stars in 1977. Out beyond our solar system, many thousand years from now, someone could retrieve the recording and hear Glenn Gould's Bach. When I listen to the *Goldberg Variations,* I'm overwhelmed by the complexity and speed of Bach's music (I prefer Gould's famous youthful version; he made a second recording of the *Variations* near the end of his career), but the C major prelude, now aboard the Voyager, is an elegantly simple piece, with slightly varied repetitions. When I first heard it, I thought, *I can learn that.*

The weather darkens up, and we spend the morning in Blue Hill. Buckwheat pancakes and bacon and real orange juice at the Left Bank Café, and then a visit to the Bagaduce Lending Library. Sheet music. Shelf after shelf of sheet music. Choral arrangements, four-handed piano, anything a music teacher or choir director would need. There are several women around this morning just helping to keep track of it all. Thousands of people, I'm told, have donated their private libraries, and the collections are safe here, in green acid-free archival boxes—and available; the music is loaned out to members. I sign up, for ten dollars. They'll soon send me a catalog of all the solo piano pieces they have. "Were you interested in anything special?" a retired piano teacher asks.

"Well, I'd just like to *see* the music for 'Träumerei.' I've been listening to it, and I'd like to see it on the page."

She comes back with two different transcriptions. The music looks daunting; I had thought it was easier.

"What's that symbol there at the bottom that looks like a snowflake?"

"It's a pedal release marking," she says.

"Oh, yes, that makes sense. What do you call it?"

She smiles and says, "A snowflake."

On the way out I notice a card tacked up on the bulletin board: PIANO FOR SALE. STEINWAY S, 1936 MODEL. BETTY BEATTY'S PIANO.

There's no sailing this weekend; the weather radio says close to ten inches of rain have fallen. We go for long walks with Will and dry him off with a towel when we get back. I'm reading Gretel Ehrlich's new book *A Match to the Heart*. I met her once and admired her writing, about life on a Wyoming ranch, and was horrified to learn that she'd been struck by lightning. We had lunch in Washington a year ago, and she told me what happened; she was still recovering, still being treated in California. Sometime her speech was hesitant. She had been out walking in the approach of an August thunderstorm. It was blowing in fast, but it looked harmless, she writes. And then: "I awoke in a pool of blood, lying on my stomach some distance from where I should have been, flung at an odd angle to one side of the dirt path.

160

The whole sky had grown dark. Was it evening, and if so, which one? How many minutes or hours had elapsed since I lost consciousness, and where were the dogs? Had I been shot in the back? Had I suffered a stroke or heart attack?" But then thunder came again, and she knew she'd been hit by lightning; the electricity, she writes, "had carved its blue path toward me." Gretel was treated ineptly in the hospital; her heart had been severely damaged, but no one paid much attention; her husband left her alone to go off and buy cattle. She credits her parents for saving her life; they sent a plane and took her home to California, and experts. The book is about her treatment, and her new life in Santa Barbara, and Sam, one of the herding dogs from the ranch, a kelpie, an Australian breed. At Christmastime she still had difficulty standing; she couldn't manage to set the table for the family dinner. On New Year's Eve, she writes:

The chest pain and light-headedness was so bad I went to bed at eight. Sam's body was pressed against mine. Did I really need anything else, anyone else in the world? At midnight I woke, stirring to the faint noise of firecrackers, looked at the clock, rolled over and kissed Sam. I wondered less about if I was going to die than if I was already dead, but my body told me otherwise: my whole left side felt as if something had been detonated there. I wanted to be held, to be pieced back together and fastened to the realm of the living by another human being, but there was no one, and there would be no one in the morning.

I have moments of sudden fear, reading this book, thinking about sailing in high winds or when the phone rings too early in the morning. I think back to the moment of impact when I slammed off my bicycle onto the wet blacktop. Or the scenes in Neenah's radio stories from Sarajevo, when she's out on the streets during the shelling and sniper fire and I know she hasn't worn the bulletproof vest. Stay with the piano, I tell myself. It can get tough, stumbling on through life; it's nice to have something that's secure and rewarding and risky only to your ego.

Our last days in Maine are comforting. Some good mornings sailing on Penobscot Bay, getting more adventurous. We walk a three-mile loop through the woods, usually seeing an eagle, sometimes a porcupine, once a bear. We have a shiatsu massage and promise next year to do it on the *first* day we arrive. We go to an Autumn Supper at the Brooksville Community Center, for roast turkey. And we cook dinner for some friends, with lamb and roasted peppers and wild applesauce. Afterward we all sit by the fire and watch two hours of the Ken Burns baseball series on PBS.

I start listening to *Morning Edition* and *All Things Considered* again and finding excuses to be in town, where I can pick up the *New York Times*. Neenah faxes off a résumé to the U.S. Holocaust Memorial Museum in Washington; people there have called her about a research assignment. A good friend's father has died; Neenah will go off to the funeral in Minnesota as soon as we get back. Our drive home is quiet. I try listening to some piano music on the way—Horowitz and George Winston—but my mind skitters off and won't listen. We arrive at our house with a new, now slightly scratched sailboat on top of the car, a well-rested dog, and a few less worries. But I've lost another month with the piano. I sit down and try to play "Misty" from memory, but most of it's gone.

OCTOBER

Salvation at a music camp, but they make me play in front of people

IT'S FRIDAY MORNING, AND I HAVE A 1:25 P.M. FLIGHT TO Albany, New York. The Autumn Sonata in Bennington runs ten days, from Friday evening through the next Sunday morning. Seems a bit long. And I'm wary of the social aspect. I already have enough friends; I can't even take care of the ones I've got. I just want to learn piano.

The morning starts moving at an anxious pace, and I make it worse by drinking too much coffee and reading the papers too fast and then deciding to find the sheet music for "Träumerei"; it would be nice to be able to play it for Neenah when I return from Vermont. I need a metronome too, a small windup one. Thirty minutes' drive to a music store. No "Träumerei." I see a metronome that might work, but it seems expensive at fifty-five dollars, and it's purple. Another music store: A clerk knows of "Träumerei," but it's out of stock. The same metronome is $49.95 here, but it's black and I can't decide. Now I'm late to start packing, and I rush home, where Neenah recognizes predeparture anxiety and offers to help. She'll make sure I have everything and take me over to National Airport.

At Albany I realize I haven't reserved a rental car, and it's a mistake I'll pay for. The National small Pontiac is $215 a week plus lots of taxes. It's an hour's drive to Bennington, and I try to make it longer. And remind myself, slowly: This is a wonderful *opportunity*. A *vacation*, and a chance to *learn*. I think I'm worried that it's hopeless, that I'm not going to have any ability for the piano after all. "Sorry," they'll say, about midweek, "the faculty has determined, Mr. Adams, that you are devoid of potential. You should leave now. There are no refunds."

Just at five o'clock I come to the Vermont state line and pull the car over and stop. *All Things Considered* is coming on the radio; I turn it off. I don't want to worry about the world, and I don't want to worry about our program. There are farms by both sides of the road. Silky white milkweed pods are blowing. The fields have been mowed, with dark, rolled bales of hay waiting. The air smells yeasty, like fermenting apples.

In Bennington I check into a motel. The rates are

high; it's "high leaf" season. The Autumn Sonata package does include room and board, but I'm a very light sleeper, and I'm worried about being in a room with three men and bunk beds. I'll stay someplace else for the first couple of nights just to be sure. I take a shower and then go find the van der Lindes' house at 5 Catamount Lane. It's in Old Bennington, on a hillside above the town. It's a white frame house with a graceful ramble to it, forty-two rooms, I've read, with enough space out back to hold summertime concerts. The van der Lindes moved here after they started teaching in earnest, and they started teaching to make sure their five children would have a good time learning.

I'm met at the door by Wayne, one of the Sonata students; he's from St. Paul, Minnesota. He introduces me to Frances, who's from Winnipeg, Manitoba, and the three of us talk for a while on the glassed-in back porch. Other people are off in the kitchen. Wayne takes me upstairs to show me room 33, where I'm supposed to be staying. A small room, two sets of bunk beds; a young man is asleep on the top of one.

I have a glass of wine and talk with Harry, who looks to be past seventy, uses a cane, and has a soft Texas accent; he's from the town of Wimberly. He's practically a beginner and tells me, "People say you'll get more in a week here than in a year of lessons."

I meet two people from Washington, D.C., Nancy, from Capitol Hill, and Charles, who lives near Dupont

Circle. I talk with Connie, a piano teacher from San Leandro, California, who's enrolled in the Sonata. "You want to play 'Träumerei'? Oh, if you can play that, you can play anything." She says she likes the idea of my having taken a computer course. The sleeping man from upstairs comes down. His name is Mark. He's a jazz player from Highlands Ranch, Colorado, who doesn't read music and has never tried a classical piece. There's some cheese and more wine and mushrooms stuffed with crab and continuing swirls of conversation: "What are you playing?" "Haydn sonatas." "Are you still playing that étude?"

Beris, from Paradise, California, is past eighty years old, strong-looking with short white hair. She's talking with Rein van der Linde, the father in this musical household. He's retired from his Bennington College career, teaching mathematics, but music has been his real love, and he still gives private piano and organ lessons. "What do you play?" Mr. van der Linde asks Beris.

"The Mozart Concerto in D Minor," she answers quickly, and adds, "I've been listening to Rudolph Serkin play it, on a CD."

He's dead, Rein mentions. Serkin died at eighty-three. "I'd take that," Rein says, "you know that's a good life."

"Oh, well—" Beris shakes her head.

Rein says, "Oh, but you see I have leukemia. I won't have that long."

Another woman, listening, says, "You look good, though, Rein. You don't look any different from two years ago."

"Well, I rest a lot." And he adds, "The treatment is worse than the disease. I give myself injections every day," making a gesture toward his leg. "Interferon."

I meet Julieanne, the cook, in the kitchen, and she tells me the beer's kept in a refrigerator out in the garage. Long Trail ale, brewed in Vermont. There's a piano in the garage, amid the bikes and skis and ladders. An old upright, but it sounds pretty good, and if the garage were heated, I'd be happy just to practice here so the others couldn't hear me. Most of this house's forty-two rooms have pianos; there's even one in a telephone closet.

An investment adviser, Richard, comes in from New York City, still wearing a coat and tie. He's brought a bottle of good gin. There's a martini shaker and a jar of olives waiting. There are twenty-three students in all. More than half the people have been here before; some come every fall. We're reminded at dinner—pasta with clam sauce, and broccoli—that the veterans should help the newcomers find their way around. There's a posted schedule of practice rooms and special classes, plus daily chores; tomorrow night at this time I'll be washing pots and pans.

I leave the house quietly, feeling that I'm sneaking out. Dinner was late; I'm tired of talking. I drive down to the motel and take a hot bath and read some of the new Ridley Pearson thriller I've brought along as a diversion—eight more days of piano to come.

SATURDAY: Arrive at Catamount Lane at 8:45 A.M. for cereal and a bagel. A few people sit quietly around a long wooden table in the kitchen; the kitchen has a big fireplace next to the stove, and positioned between the fireplace and the stove is an almost permanent dog, a black Lab named Tycho, lying on his bed.

I feel a bit more comfortable this morning. I realize I arrived at the Autumn Sonata with a deep dread of having to stand up in a room full of strangers and say my name and hometown and what my piano experience has been and what pieces I was playing and, worst of all, what I hoped to accomplish during my time here. There would be smiles and polite applause. (I used to help teach radio production workshops around the country and always at the first session we'd ask the reporters to stand and tell us why they wanted to attend. I found myself hating the phrase "to hone my skills." Several people would say it; you could always hear it coming.) But the Sonata began without ceremony, and then I became very curious about the other people. Who indeed were they? How well could they play? How much did they practice? How did they find the time? Why did they come here?

Another van der Linde has arrived in the night; Polly's driven up from her home in New Jersey. Her mother, Rosamond, runs the Sonata, with Rein helping as much as he can. Polly's younger brother, Tiaan, is here, and sisters Tasha and Erica are coming later. Any van der Linde you meet can teach you piano, but Polly had a special reputation. "She's the best," several of the veteran campers agree.

I check the practice schedule and take a cup of coffee upstairs to room 21. It's one of the women's bedrooms. Three bunk beds, suitcases, a couple of chairs—and a piano. A Kawai upright, sitting on an uneven floor so the keyboard slants a little from the treble to the bass.

I play "Misty." I've shut the door, but I can still hear the piano in the next room, something classical and smooth. I can hear a distant thunder of chords from down the hall. Perhaps someone will wander past and hear my playing and say, "Hey, sounds like a jazz guy warming up." I play on and daydream, hoping the door will open and the next part of my music life will begin. The lessons are unscheduled. The teachers will just show up in the morning or afternoon or both, and suddenly you'll have an hourlong lesson.

My back starts aching, and I take the excuse to quit and go downstairs. There's a sight-reading class in the living room, advice on playing new music at first glance. Pay attention to the title of the piece, we're told, for hints about the character of the music. Find a tempo that's slow enough. Watch the music, not the keyboard. And the most important thing: "Always choose pieces that are easier than the ones you are actually learning."

This is a problem for me since at the moment I'm not actually learning anything.

For lunch there's put-it-together-yourself sandwiches, ham and Vermont cheddar cheese, some leftover broccoli from last night. Then I find the music library downstairs—shelves and cabinets full of sheet music. "Träumerei" is here; it looks just as hard as it did when I saw it last month in Maine. I also sign the borrower's clipboard for a book of hymns with only three chords and an arrangement of "Misty." I'm tired of looking at those black dot and white dot chord charts in David Sudnow's instruction manual, and it's nice to see what the real music looks like.

I do, however, have to show the Sudnow "Misty" chart to a teacher just an hour later, back in room 21 at the left-leaning Kawai. Mary Beth walks in. "How about a lesson?" she says brightly. She spots "Misty" on the music rack. "What is that? I've never seen anything like that before." I explain about the learn-jazz-by-ear course and play some of the song for her. I play it badly. She's not impressed. I explain about the computer course and show her some sheet music I've brought from home—"Bridge over Troubled Water" and "Tears in Heaven"—and tell her that I've had little time to practice. "What's your goal for this week?" she asks. "What about Saturday?" There's a recital at the end of the Sonata for everyone who'd like to play.

I say with some confidence, "I'd like to learn 'Träumerei.' "

Her response is a quiet "Ooooh."

"Well, let's look at it," she says. I start playing and get stuck at a chord in the second measure. The right thumb crosses over the left thumb? Is that it? I manage to figure out a couple of grace notes in measure three. Measure four is far beyond me. Mary Beth continues on, though, singing the music down through the end of the first section where the repeat begins. "You know about repeats?" she asks. "These lines and the four dots? See, they match up with the lines and dots back at the beginning of measure two. You just play the next eight measures again and then go on with the piece."

We talk some about intervals. Do I see them in the music? Notes that are a third of an octave apart? A fifth? It's a way of learning to read music by patterns, without bothering to name the notes. The thumb and second fingers play a third; the thumb and fourth fingers fit naturally over a fourth. And Mary Beth notices that my left hand seems uncoordinated and weak. This is in part because I'm right-handed, but also I've not been playing much with the left; all the scale training in the Sudnow course is for the right hand only. "Here's Hanon," she says, pulling a page of sheet music out of her bag. I see that notes for both hands are marching up and down the keyboard: "Preparatory exercises for the acquirement of agility, independence, strength and perfect evenness in the fingers."

"About 'Träumerei'?" she says. "It's really hard, it's probably a third-year piece, and while I respect your determination, maybe it's best if you have something else to learn, something to fall back on for Saturday's recital." She finds some more music in her bag. "Why don't you try this Bach prelude?" And she plays through the piece for me. It's the Prelude in C Major from *The Well-Tempered Clavier*—our old friend from the Glenn Gould Voyager recording.

Mary Beth leaves me with a lot of music in my mind. I should be able to learn the Bach prelude in time for the recital. She's shown me how to practice it in block chords, playing three notes in each hand. But I also— cautiously—try the first measures of "Träumerei." The chords that I manage to find are lovely and gratifying. Later, at the motel, I fall asleep listening to folk music from WAMC in Albany: Mary Black singing "The Urge for Going" and Cheryl Wheeler's "When Fall Comes to New England."

SUNDAY: Much talk at breakfast about last night's dessert, "Better than Sex Cake (chocolate)," said to be a Sonata favorite. I usually stay away from chocolate and had managed to pass. And somehow there is a connection between the dessert and a piano joke, a man-goes-into-a-bar story, which involves a tiny piano and a tiny man to play it and has this punchline: "You don't think I asked for a twelve-inch *pianist,* do you?"

My morning practice is on a digital keyboard set up in a hallway, playing with headphones. It's a Roland keyboard, and it has a pretty good touch. When you play the Hanon exercises, you can easily leave the music behind, with your hands just moving along the keyboard without conscious thought. It's sort of like what happens when you run several miles. You could probably even read or listen to the radio while playing Hanon; wouldn't do your musical mind much good, but your fingers would surely get stronger. "Play Hanon twenty minutes a day, it's great," one of my Sonatamates says.

"Do you do it?" I ask.

"Nope."

Mary Beth has also given me a couple of scales to play and, along with my wandering through the beginning of "Träumerei," it's enough to keep busy, but I'm distracted by the music from another room. Chords are crashing behind the door. Someone walks by and says, "Can you believe that's Beris? She's eighty years old. It sounds like a powerful man in there."

In the late afternoon there's a master class in the living room. Polly's the teacher, stationed at a big Kawai grand. A master class sounded fine to me, but I'm not sure what it is, and I'm apprehensive because Polly's asked me to play a few notes of Mozart. Karen plays first, though, and she is superconfident. She's from Minot, North Dakota, has perfect pitch and a Steinway B in her front room. Karen starts the Chopin ballade that she's been working on. Polly listens closely, then stops her to make suggestions about phrasing, talking both to Karen and to the class. "Try it that way, try it again,"

Polly says, and now even I can tell the difference. It's like a magic trick, and there's a gasp from the people in the room. Karen is glowing.

Soon it's my turn, and there's applause because, Polly tells the class, this is the first time I've played before an audience. I have only a few notes to play for Polly's demonstration, and I do, indeed, play the phrase better after her coaching. I'm shaky-nervous, but it goes well, and again there's applause; it's a pretty supportive bunch I'm with here.

I have a talk later with Karen and with Sandy about Polly's teaching. Sandy's trying to figure out a way that Polly can come down to Washington and teach several of us on the same day and possibly play a recital as well. Karen's frustrated because North Dakota and Polly are too far apart. She also appreciates Polly's playing skills. "There are some music teachers," Karen says, "who can't find 'Happy Birthday' on the piano. If they were at a party, they wouldn't be able to play it."

Sandy says it's important to have something ready when people ask you to play the piano. Your family makes sacrifices, your friends know you take lessons and practice, you shouldn't be shy about playing, you should always have something worked up. "What do you play when they ask?" I wonder.

"Oh, one of Mendelssohn's *Songs Without Words*, one of those."

In the evening I play "Träumerei" for an hour or so

on a old upright downstairs in the laundry room. I'm still on the first line. It doesn't make sense to try to learn this in time for Saturday's recital. I mentioned to the van der Lindes that I was thinking about "Träumerei," prompting Rosamond's wonderful laugh. She said, "Teachers and the students call it 'trauma.'"

"That's a difficult piece," Rein said. And he added, "I hope you play it better than Horowitz did." He wasn't joking.

MONDAY: "If you ask a class of five-year-olds to name a living composer, they name one in their class!" This is Rosamond van der Linde talking about children. She has the attention of seven adults this morning; it's a class that teaches you how Rosamond teaches. We'll meet for an hour every day to go through her lessons. "Kids," she says, "don't know the difference between right and left and low and high." If you ask about "high" on the piano, they'll look above it. A perfectly sensible piano to a child, Rosamond explains, would be one that is vertical, that stands on the bass end with the treble side pointing to the ceiling.

Everyone plays in Rosamond's first class, and since we're the students as well as the observers, we take up positions—two to a piano. "Get set to play a pattern on any of the black notes. Any of them, any order." She points to a team: "Start. Now you two play." And four hands, then six, then eight are all playing whatever they feel like, and it all makes sense, Rosamond tells us, because we're playing only the black keys—the pentatonic scale. We can't go wrong.

To prove it, she stands over a piano and tells a story. "A sailboat leaves the dock on a pretty day." She plays several black keys in a happy trill. "The boat sails out of the harbor and into the open water of the ocean." More black keys, a touch lower, more rhythmic. "Everybody's happy; the sailboat is cruising along." Middle of the keyboard now, still just on the black notes, a spirited rocking sound. "Then the wind picks up [keys dancing]; the waves get higher; a storm is coming fast [furious music]. And the dark sky cracks open with thunder [boom and bang of black key bass notes]. The sails strain in the wind [add higher notes, fast, then faster]. But at the most fearful moment there's one ray of sunshine through the angry clouds [a single note, like a chime]. The wind slows; the sea calms; the sailboat rides the gentle swells, turning toward home port [with all appropriate accompaniment]."

Rosamond teaches children not only that they can play a piece of music the first time they touch a keyboard but that they can also improvise. And she explains the interval training to us: one note, then up a third, a fifth, a sixth, and so on. Don't bother with the letter names of the notes; after all, you don't see the letters on the sheet music, just the notes and their relative positions. The only reason you eventually need to name the notes is so you can talk about them, so somebody can yell in from the kitchen, "No, no, it's C-sharp." Rosamond's daughter Erica, my friend at Steinway, started studying at Juilliard when she was twelve. She could play, she could read music, but when she went to her first class in New York, she didn't know the names of the notes.

And Rosamond remembers what she used to yell out the window at Polly, playing with her friends. Instead of saying, "Come on in, it's time to practice," it was "Bring your friends in; we're going to have some fun at the piano."

Rosamond van der Linde believes that electronic keyboards are great for the piano teaching business. Parents will buy one and play around; it's cheap, it's fun. Give it to the kids or throw it in the closet and buy a better one. Many people, Rosamond says, go on to buy acoustic pianos. And often several people in the family are learning at the same time. Especially boys now—her classes are half boys, but they used to be mostly girls. Traditionally piano lessons were thought of as "refining school." And what could be simpler than learning piano? Learn the location of one single note—an F—and just look at how far away the other notes are. You can figure it out by looking at the keyboard and the music. But the sessions have to be fun and challenging and productive, or else, Rosamond reminds us, "you're stuck in John Thompson for a year, or you play 'Für Elise' for a year, then quit."

"The Leaf" shows up just before lunchtime. It's out

on the back lawn, dancing. We hear music and people laughing and go outside and find a young woman dressed in brown tights and a large foam rubber leaf. There's a tape player on the ground and she's cavorting around to the "Maple Leaf Rag," spinning and hopping and rolling on the grass in the real leaves. It seems to be a Bennington sort of thing.

After a ham sandwich and cider I spend the afternoon at a piano. I'm supposed to have found a partner and started to learn a duet for Saturday's recital. I could sign up for something called the "Monster Concert," also on Saturday. But I'm convinced "Träumerei" can be my piano salvation. Who cares about all the frustrating months if I can learn an important piece of music? Elizabeth, another student from Washington, D.C., mentioned at lunch that she'd heard about the Russians' love for "Träumerei." It was obvious from the videotape of the Horowitz Moscow concert, and she said that the song is played at the World War II memorial at Volgograd. Music by a German composer played to honor the bravery of Russian soldiers killed by Germans.

I warm up with thirty minutes of the Hanon exercises and then start "Träumerei," trying to figure out the fourth measure. A new teacher, Bonnie, opens the door. I quickly recite my piano history for her, ending with my hope to play the Schumann piece by Saturday. Bonnie smiles softly and says that playing "Träumerei" at my level is like trying to climb Mount Everest. Schumann didn't write any easy music, she says. And she mentions that I should talk with Rein. Schumann is his favorite composer. In the living room the van der Lindes have a shelf of books about music and composers. I've checked on Robert Schumann, and it seems bleak: He started learning piano at six, first appeared in concert at seventeen, hurt one of his fingers through faulty practicing, gave up performing, became a composer, married a pianist, had severe nervous disorders, and died in an asylum.

Bonnie suggests, with a laugh, that I could substitute "Misty" for "Träumerei," since I can already sort of play it and the titles mean the same thing (you'll see *Träumerei* translated as "reverie" or "dreaming"). But then she runs downstairs to the music library and returns with a photocopy of a Robert Vandall piece, Prelude no. 7 in B Minor. "Let's try this," she says, opening the pages and sitting beside me on the bench. "This is lovely; it has a 'Moonlight Sonata' feel. I give this to my students, and they take two weeks to learn it."

She plays through the short piece. The left hand has repeating bass figures, and the right plays a rolling melody. Later, when I try to play it by myself, I get lost, and it takes me a long time to figure out that both the top staff and the bottom are in the bass clef; the right hand is playing below middle C. Then it's normal for eight measures before both hands move up to the treble clef. The Vandall prelude goes into my music bag alongside the Bach. Now I have two pieces of music that I can't play, plus "Träumerei."

TUESDAY: In the evening near dusk, after two long sessions at the piano, it's good to get out in the clean, wet air. I go for a run, quickly up out of town and on into the country along a road leading to the airport. There are yellow roses surviving against the warmth of a stone wall, facing south. I try to run faster, breathing deeply to get some moisture into my body. I'm feeling less anxious, having decided it doesn't make sense to try to crash on through "Träumerei" by Saturday. But there's some guilt involved. Sometimes I'm afraid that I approach the piano the way I approach running: I've been in a few races, but I've never *really* pushed myself, never tried to find out how fast and how far I could run. And some days at NPR I feel as if I'm only half there. When I have no choice but to focus on the work—the intense week in Northern Ireland is a good example—there's always satisfaction when it's over.

On the way back to Catamount Lane I stop at the old graveyard at the Congregational Church and walk among the lichen-dappled headstones, noticing the unusual Christian names. Noahdiah is my favorite. And there's Alpheus, and Lavinda, and Cebra (Quakenbush). Revolutionary soldiers are buried here. And so is Robert Frost (1874–1963). His wife, Elinor, is with him; she died in 1938. There are two small birch trees at their gravesite, which is in the shadow of a lovely old oak, now with yellow leaves. The markers are limestone, and there's an inscription (from a Frost poem): "Together wing to wing and oar to oar."

"Learn to play 'Träumerei' as a Christmas present," Rosamond van der Linde told me earlier. "Play it for your wife and surprise her." I was practicing in the laundry room when the door banged open, and there was Rosamond, laughing. She couldn't find the person she was supposed to teach so she just started opening doors until she came to an unaccompanied student. "How about a lesson?"

But first we talked about what I was learning and how I thought things were going. She asked to hear the Hanon exercises and noticed that I wasn't lifting my fingers high enough. Play it slowly, she said, deliberately, to build strength. Play with a big tone and "no hangovers," meaning notes that aren't being released in time for the next one to sound clearly. At the top of a blank page in my practice notebook she wrote, about my playing, "Nice steady beat." She also said I had terrific hands for the piano and wrote that down: "Terrific equipment!" I was so surprised I didn't think to ask what she meant.

Keep playing Hanon, she said. Yes, the Vandall piece would be great to learn. Keep the Bach prelude on a back burner. "And let's just see about 'Träumerei.'" She closed the cover over the keyboard. "Play the notes on the wood." And she sang the melody along with my silent playing; she wanted me to learn the rhythm of the first four measures without having to worry about striking the right notes. She sang and counted; I played. And again. She divided the measures with quick pencil strokes, showing where the beats fall. Then Rosamond *deconstructed* the four measures for me, as if to say, you know this music can get pretty complicated. "This is a song," she explained. "And you hear four voices. These top notes are the soprano; that's the melody. Those notes just under the soprano are for the alto voice, and then in the left hand, the baritone and bass." Suddenly I could see the four harmony lines. We took the time to play them separately, singing and counting along the way (now I'm beginning to understand why Glenn Gould didn't worry about being quiet when he played).

Then I tried the four parts together, with both hands. I played badly—overwhelmed by the complexity of just this first line of "Träumerei." I'm lost in a new world, and I'm still at the very top of the page. "If you really have to play it," Rosamond said, "then go ahead. I've learned it's best to let people try because there's a reason they have such a connection to a piece of music." But then she mentioned it might be best to learn the piece as a Christmas present, and it seemed just right to do that: to play it for Neenah on Christmas Eve. It was a great relief.

I get back after my run in time for a long shower before dinner. We're having ham tonight, and Julieanne has made mashed potatoes, blending in cream cheese and whipping it all with half-and-half. With a good meal and some wine after a day of playing and learning, I feel just a little bit like a pianist. "No," I say to the others, "we've decided to leave the Schumann for a while, and I'll learn the Vandall piece for Saturday."

WEDNESDAY: Wake up in a peach-colored room at a bed-and-breakfast called the South Shire Inn, near the center of town. I thought the Hobbit connection would be good luck, so I moved from the motel. Somehow Bennington makes you think of rereading your favorite books, and there's a used bookstore with plenty of J. R. R. Tolkien and Frost and Zane Grey. The inn is lovely—I especially like the lighting in the bathroom; it makes me look happy and rested—but in truth, it's too upscale for my needs this week. I realize I could have brought a sleeping bag and a tent and been quite comfortable out in the van der Lindes' backyard. Could take my showers inside (although I did hear someone joking about standing in line to get in a bathroom at 4:30 A.M.).

My friend Erica has arrived from New York, and it's great to see her. She's borrowed a couple of days from her job at Steinway to come up and help her parents with the Autumn Sonata. She's in jeans and a sweater, looks happy. It's been a good year she says; she's Steinway's leading salesperson so far.

"Have you heard Tori Amos play?" I ask, especially

because Tori Amos plays a Bösendorfer and Erica used to sell those pianos.

"No," she says, "but have *you* heard Jacky Terrasson? A young jazz pianist? He's signed with Blue Note. He's fantastic."

Erica asks after my piano: "How's it doing?" I tell her about the humidity problems and the discouraging times I had in late summer when even a concert grand Steinway wouldn't have been inspiring. Erica says she's not been playing much for years now—just too much piano in her life—but this fall she fell in love with one particular Model M. In mahogany. And her eyes gleamed when she told me about the strength and grace of the low notes and the piano's long sustain—the lasting power of the notes. It's amazing that factory-built instruments could be so different that one piano could speak so directly to one person. She didn't buy it, but she was very pleased with the people who eventually did. A mother and dad and their young daughter, who was obviously talented and who loved the piano's sound and touch.

I had asked Erica's mother, Rosamond, about her all-time favorite piano. "It's in room nine," she said. "A Steinway. It was given to me as a college graduation present and had been in the family for a long time. My aunt bought it at the Chicago World's Fair in 1893."

There's a group outing for lunch today; everyone's going into town to eat at a friendly-looking place called Alldays & Onions. I decide to stay behind and make a peanut butter sandwich and practice. Every day there's some sort of non-piano activity: a museum visit, a shopping trip. And there's far more sitting around and talking time in the evenings than I need. But I'm surely in the antisocial minority. People do make lasting friends here and look forward to seeing them each fall.

I go to Rosamond's class for teachers at 10:30 A.M., where we learn how to find all the notes in a given major scale, counting upward from the key signature note, moving in whole steps from white note to the next white note, and half steps, from the white note to the next black note. I've covered most of this in the Sudnow course, back in the summer. We also learn more than twenty different ways to play the Hanon exercises. In odd rhythms, at varying speeds, and my favorite: contrary motion, with both thumbs starting together.

The afternoon is spent alone, playing the Bach prelude and working on the difficult middle section of the the Vandall prelude. The Vandall is improving, and I don't think I'll totally embarrass myself on Saturday. There was talk today among the men students. Walter, a Sonata veteran from San Francisco, said it's customary to dress up for the recital, to wear a coat and tie. Although maybe it's time to change that, he wondered. I'm for tradition, I said, remembering that I brought a blue blazer.

I also practice "Träumerei," for old times' sake. Rosamond has brought me the music in a two-page edition. On the single page the notes are jammed up close together, the staves are dense with music; you'll look down at the keyboard to find the right note, and when you look back up, you've lost your place. On two pages —this is an Alfred edition—the piece opens up and makes more visual sense. Now it almost looks playable. I'll have to get my own copy at home. The van der Lindes' "Träumerei" has penciled fingering notes— "Erica's," Rosamond said, "from years ago, when she was learning it."

THURSDAY: A sign on the students' bulletin board says: "Whether you learn to sight-read the Chopin 'Polonaise' or not, you're out of here at nine A.M." This is a warning about Sunday morning. We'll have the recital Saturday afternoon, a big celebration dinner that night, and everyone's expected to be on his or her way back home by nine Sunday morning. That's when the fifteen pianos stop and the van der Lindes get their house back. I wonder what they do, the first hours after we're gone. Most likely it's coffee and the Sunday papers and later a quiet time to play piano—alone.

I'd heard that Rein van der Linde was fond of sailing and talked with him one evening. "Do you sail?" he said. "I love it." He told me of a late-summer mishap with his new nineteen-foot catboat, on the Nova Scotia coast. A nor'easter was coming; they'd left the boat on a mooring in a safe harbor, but it broke loose during the storm and wrecked on the rocks. A few thousand to fix it, he guessed. But he will. I asked if he'd ever thought of a relationship between sailing and music. Both allow you to escape a daily world, to dream? A wooden sailboat is much like a piano, handcrafted, as pretty at rest as in performance? "No." He shook his head. "I wouldn't have said that. I do think there's a great connection between music and mathematics."

Between music and all the sciences, I suppose. Two of our more accomplished students here are radiologists, friends from Los Angeles. One of them, Carol, plays in an all-physicians' orchestra there. Harry, the older fellow from Texas, told me he'd been in the oil business. He's come very late to the piano and he's had a stroke, but he seems to be doing fine. "I've finished the second Alfred book," he told me. Alfred is a music publishing company with a popular series of adult piano instruction books. If he's now on the third Alfred book, he's far ahead of me. I've seen Harry walking into town for exercise, moving slowly, bent over his cane, a step at a time. His wife is coming at week's end, and they'll go on over to Maine for a vacation at an Elderhostel. When I drive past Harry on the hill going into town, I worry about myself: Why can't I take time to sit down and talk with him? Find out about his life and why he cares so much about the piano.

I'm playing so much now that there's a painful knot in the back of my shoulder near the spine. No amount of stretching seems to touch it. And I find myself slumping on the piano bench; how do pianists manage to sit up straight all that time? My hands feel stronger, because I'm playing the Hanon exercises every day, but I suspect that finger strength is really not that important to older beginners. We are a long way from playing something that will challenge our physical abilities. There's a moment, though, in "Träumerei" that presents a stretch. It's a big, showy two-handed chord near the end; the reach is ten notes in each hand. I'm realizing now I have fairly big hands (my height is only five feet five inches) and can manage—a touch painfully—to play this chord. It's a satisfying feeling and a great sound.

I have a lesson with Leslie in a tiny room below the main staircase. The piano is a Kawai upright. "Let's get ready for the recital," Leslie says. I open the green book of Vandall preludes and turn to no. 7 in B minor. I play slowly, missing notes, but not without some feeling. As a professional teacher Leslie has no choice but to say, when I come to the end, "If this is your debut, this is just fine. You can be proud of this." Then the teaching starts. "What happens on the radio when you make a mistake, when you say something wrong, what do you do?" I explain that if no factual error is involved, I just go on as if nothing had happened. "Exactly," Leslie says. "And a note isn't a fact, so just go on past it. If you try to fix it, you'll also be making a mistake in rhythm, and you'll just be telling the audience, 'Hey, I messed up.' The audience doesn't know what the notes are anyway, usually." Another teacher told me earlier,

"Play the wrong notes firmly, with as much confidence as you play the correct ones."

I ask Leslie what I should be doing just at the moment when it's time to start playing. She explains that it's okay to place your hands on the keys before you play and that you should think about tempo and how the first phrases should sound. She's noticed I'm *striking* the notes in the right hand, playing the thumb and third and fifth fingers individually. "Roll the hand," she says. And demonstrates, letting her hand turn with the notes. "Let your elbow move with it too." I've seen pianists play with a lot of arm movement and always thought it was an affectation, just for show, but I try the opening measures letting my elbow float and rolling my right hand, and the notes do respond; they sound as if they belong together.

"Let's go in the living room and play on the big piano," Leslie suggests. *Oooh,* I think. This is where Saturday's recital will be. It's the Kawai grand and one that many of the students dislike; it sounds fine, but the action is slow and you really have to be *playing* this piano, they say. "Wait," Leslie says, "let me introduce you." And I sit in a chair where the audience will be, and Leslie stands in front and announces my name and the piece I'll be playing and then applauds as I come up to the piano. I sit and wait, fingers over the opening chord, then begin. The action is difficult; some of my notes are barely audible. I finish, and Leslie claps and comes over to sit beside me on the bench. She says I'll adjust to this piano if I play it some more, that your hands have muscle memory, they can remember how every key feels.

I start the piece again as Leslie goes off to another lesson. And Karen comes in; she's the really good pianist from North Dakota. "Mind if I listen?" she asks. And I don't really because I think if you keep on being afraid to play for people, it could only get worse. So I play the prelude for Karen and relax a bit and start to feel an emotional connection with the music. It must be that I'm finally concentrating enough. I talk with Karen about this, saying that it often happens on the radio that you'll read a script without the proper attention, or writing that you don't understand, and you'll sound phony. Karen smiles. "Of course that's true." And she says, "Playing for someone is like giving them a gift."

There's fun in the kitchen before dinner with a nifty old-fashioned apple peeler. Plenty of volunteers to work it: You stick the apple on a spike, line up the blade, and keep on cranking as the peel spins off. Another motion and the apple's cored, ready for one of the three pie dishes that Julieanne's set out. I get down on the floor next to Tycho, the big Lab that is really Tiaan van der Linde's dog. Tycho isn't allowed out of the kitchen, Tiaan tells me (sometimes when his parents are gone, Tiaan will let the dog run through the rest of the house just to watch him get excited). I lie close to Tycho and rub my hand down the length of his spine; with more than twenty students around he gets plenty of dropped tidbits, but obviously not much physical affection. He groans and rolls closer. After I'm away from home for about a week, I always have to get my hands on a dog.

I phone Neenah to see how things are going. She sounds lonely, says she's opening two cans at supper-time, one for her and one for the dogs. Both Will and Bonny are sleeping in our bedroom. Bonny's on the bed, but Will can't make the jump anymore. But the *news* is that Šejla, Neenah's interpreter friend, has ar-rived from Sarajevo by way of Vienna. Neenah went to pick her up at Dulles Airport, and they've had a grand reunion. It's going to be an interesting time of adjust-ment. Šejla Bezdrob (pronounced SHAY-luh BEZ-drob) has left her parents and sister behind in a city at war. In January she'll enroll as a junior at the American Univer-sity in Washington, studying journalism. An AU staff member arranged for Šejla's visa and has offered a place to stay until she gets settled. Many people have helped with money and months of phone calls and faxes.

FRIDAY: An early start—I have breakfast duty, making sure all the different cereal boxes are set out and the orange juice is made and the coffee's ready. I stop on the way up to Catamount Lane for a dozen hot bagels. I also bring the *New York Times*, and I think I shouldn't have. Richard takes the business section, someone else wants the weekend pages, and the breakfast dynamic seems to change. Suddenly we aren't piano people anymore.

Practice for an hour after breakfast. Then it's time for Rosamond's final teacher's class. She introduces us to the fake book; it's what musicians use when they have to play a song they don't know. "Want to play cocktail piano," Rosamond says, "pay attention." She shows us the patterns for a major chord, a minor chord, a diminished chord, and an augmented chord. Four different positions for the left hand, all within the eight notes of the octave. And the revelation: "These are the chords you use for any key." In other words, select a key, find the eight notes in that key's scale, use the four chord patterns as the left hand part—and play the melody with the right hand! The fake books—one of them is actually called *The Real Fake Book*—contain hundreds of popular songs, with the melody line printed out but just chord indications for the accompaniment. If I squint my eyes and think about this really hard, I figure I could do it. I could buy a book and someone could ask me to play "Moon River" and after an hour or so I'd have it. This is, of course, exactly what David Sudnow's course was trying to teach me, but somehow Rosamond was able to explain it better in only about three minutes.

And Rein had a class for us this morning. An organ and harpsichord workshop. Twenty-five years ago they bought a wonderful pipe organ from a nearby church. The church wanted an electric organ and sold the old one to the van der Lindes for $150; it's worth thousands now. Rein explained how the bellows worked and showed us how the various stops change the sound. And Carol, the radiologist, volunteered to join him for a piano and flute sonata played on the organ. She played the piano part, with both hands on the organ's lower keyboard, and Rein played the flute melody with one hand, on the upper keyboard. And he demonstrated the harpsichord for us, showing how a quill, the plectrum, rises to pluck each string. Beris, fearless, jumped up from her chair to play some Bach.

Out on the back lawn for a group photograph, and then almost everyone leaves for lunch and shopping in Manchester. Good outlet stores, they say. I have a lesson scheduled with Mary Beth, and the Vandall piece feels a long way from being ready.

"Your pedaling's wrong," says Mary Beth. And I realize right away that she's right. I'd thought something was slightly off with the pedaling. The sustain pedal is supposed to lift and go back down very quickly just *after* the note. I had been pedaling *right on* the note, and it's a big difference. But now, even though it sounds better, I'm in trouble. The recital is a day away, and I've got to go back through and unlearn all the pedaling. I can't practice to get better anymore; I've got to play to fix my mistakes. Mary Beth says I'll do fine.

I have another new place to sleep tonight, the Kirkside, next to a big church on Main Street. It's my favorite kind of motel. A small, very clean room. Firm mattress, even a white cotton bedspread, and a bathtub. I get in bed early and read some and listen to music on the radio. I'm nervous about tomorrow; I know how dreadful stage fright can be. Polly and I talked earlier in the week about Inderal; it's a beta-blocker, a drug used to treat some heart conditions. A lot of musicians will take Inderal to help with stage fright, especially at auditions. It's said to stop your hands from shaking. I've been hearing about Inderal for years, and I was surprised to learn that it's still popular. I can now almost play the Vandall piece all the way through without a mistake, and I'm very curious to see how the recital performance will change because of stage fright. Although adrenaline does have several good effects, I don't think it's likely I'll be playing *better* tomorrow.

Before I go to sleep, I call my mother at her home out in Ohio. "Do you think," she wonders, "those lessons you had years ago made any difference?" Those were lessons she probably couldn't afford, and I practiced on a piano she had to rent. You bet it made a difference, I tell her.

SATURDAY: Take the deepest of breaths and watch for a tremble; the recital is about to begin. Rosamond stands in front of the piano and says, "We have something special for you. Rein is going to play; it's for someone in the audience."

And the maestro takes his place on the bench, lays

out a book of music, and smiles. "I want to play 'Träumerei,' for Noah."

His touch is strong, and sad. He plays as if remembering. It's a thrill to hear the piece being played right in front of me. Before the applause is over, Rein is up searching for his tuner's crank. One of the notes has new strings and is out of tune, badly, he says. I asked him later which note it was. "The low G. Didn't you hear it?"

Richard is the first student to perform. He asked for the honor; his brother is coming soon to pick him up for the drive back to New York. Richard is extremely nearsighted and doesn't drive. He also has difficulty reading music but today plays Rachmaninoff beautifully from memory. Honest, appreciative applause as Richard goes back to his seat, and then he stands to take another bow. Several of us, as we applaud Richard's playing, notice through the front window that a man who looks like Richard has just pulled up in a red Volvo station wagon, and I know we're all thinking, *Oh, what a shame his brother didn't get to hear him play.* But then Rosamond notices and yes, why not? "Richard, would you play the piece again?" Cheers from the audience. A wide grin on Richard's face as he begins. But as it has to be, he played it better the first time.

I'm not paying much attention, really. There's a coppery taste in my mouth, and my hands are cold. This is apparently quite common. Polly had recommended hot water. And I'd read that Glenn Gould, before a concert, would soak his hands and wrists until they were bright red.

I had designed a peaceful, pleasant morning for myself. I sat around after breakfast with coffee and the *New York Times*. Played my Vandall prelude a few times. "Don't overprepare," I was told. I can play the prelude pretty well, but I don't know how to factor in the fear. Earlier in the week I'd seen someone wearing a button that said, "I PLAYED IT BETTER AT HOME," and I now understand how that works.

And I was sure it would be relaxing to watch Leslie's eurythmics class. Leslie teaches five-year-olds, and even younger ones, every Saturday morning. They have bright looks and are hopping with energy. Their parents —these are families from the Bennington area—sit beside them on the carpet. There's a tiny girl with her thumb in her mouth who won't do much more than kick her feet in time with the music, but the others play clapping games and dance around and help Leslie at the piano sing her songs. Jaques-Dalcroze invented the eurythmics teaching method; it combines music and movement and acting—everything, it seems, that children do naturally and the rest of us painstakingly and self-consciously have to relearn.

The recital goes on: a Chopin mazurka, some Shostakovich. A mother and her daughter, both students, play a Beethoven sonata. Beris, wearing a long jade dress, plays the first movement of Bach's *Italian* Concerto.

Then there's a break for fun, as we move downstairs to a room that has four pianos. The teachers and several of the students have worked up a terrific arrangement for eight players—"The Grand Piano Band." The melody bounces back and forth among the pianos, or a phrase will start in the bass of piano number one and finish in the treble of piano number four. It's music to laugh with.

Then some quite serious madrigal singing, without piano, before a fifteen-minute intermission. It will soon be my turn to perform. I walk around in the backyard, telling myself that it's only a bit of piano playing in front of people I know and like and that I'm on the radio every evening talking to more than a million strangers. I make a cup of peppermint tea, mostly just to hold and keep my hands warm, and the recital starts again.

Harry plays the Bach prelude, the same one Mary Beth thought I might try. After shuffling to the piano without his cane, Harry says, "It's been sixty-eight years since I've done this." He smiles and plays badly, missing a third of the notes and not making much music out of the rest. Enthusiastic clapping. Helen, from Manhattan, plays Chopin; Nancy plays Mendelssohn; Mark plays jazz variations on "My Favorite Things." And Connie, the California piano teacher, does a superb job with a Debussy ballade; Rein stands up to lead the applause.

And suddenly I'm at the piano. The Kawai nine-foot grand sits sideways in an alcove formed by a large bay window. White lace curtains, creamy yellow walls. The room opens to my right, where the audience waits, sitting on folding chairs. The name of my piece has been announced, so there's really nothing for me to say. I adjust the knobs on the sides of the piano bench, raising it about an inch. I take off my glasses; with the bifocals any head movement would throw the notes out of focus. I push the wooden frame holding the music back two inches, place my foot on the right pedal, and push it down to feel the tension. My hands wait above the first notes. I hear the phrase in my mind . . . and begin.

It's like skating very, very fast on dangerous ice, being pushed by the wind with no way to slow down. I don't feel over-the-top nervous, but as I begin the graceful eleven-note run up three octaves with my right hand, it starts to shake. Drastically. I'm still playing the correct keys, I think, but it's scary to see your hand shake like that. I miss a few notes, just leaving them behind, mostly because this piano's action is so heavy, I tell myself. The middle part's coming up; I could collapse right here. I slow down for it, but I can still hear the bad notes clanging like a pinball machine. Some light, repeated phrases go okay, and then I'm thankfully into the last eight measures, which essentially repeat the opening. I bear down on the low notes, trying to find the emotion I've known playing this part. The soft ending chord comes up—I look at the keyboard, so I won't make a horrendous final mistake—and then I hold the notes for a time, taking care to release the pedal slowly.

A half hour later I'm standing in the kitchen, drinking a beer, accepting compliments. It's an *athletic* glow —an after-race satisfaction. People tell me that they were indeed moved when I played, that I had a great deal of musicality and a great touch. And the response had seemed genuine; I took an extra bow as they applauded. I could tell my face was flushed, and I had an out-of-control grin.

The week ends with a feast. Prosciutto with melon and Seckel pears with Gorgonzola for appetizers, roast turkey and dressing, and then pumpkin pie with ice cream. And piano stories among piano players.

NOVEMBER

> *A Vermont guy who loves free pianos and
> a New York teacher who adores Steinways*

A RETURN HOME TO COLD, RAINY WEATHER, THE LEAVES
mostly down, the sailboat waiting undercover as the season hesitates. I came back from Vermont with a three-
pound wheel of cheddar cheese, five white dinner plates
(seconds) from Bennington Potters, and a desire to play
the piano— immediately—for Neenah. She'd hoped the
weather would be clear enough to sail after she picked
me up at National Airport; I just wanted to play the
Vandall prelude. I'd asked Elizabeth, a fellow student,
on the flight down to Washington from Albany if she
intended to go straight home and play her recital piece.
She laughed. "Sure, that's what everybody does."

My piano seems stubborn, the keys unfamiliar. Neenah listens politely. "That's wonderful," she says. But I'm missing notes and have to start again. I relax some and then play the piece through twice. I'm just amazed at this need to perform, and I think Neenah is a little mystified as well. There's a logic to it that I understand —if you play a lot for people, it becomes a less frightening proposition—but I think of myself as a much shyer person. "How can he say that?" a voice asks, inside my mind. "Isn't this the same guy who put on dark glasses at the end of his *Good Evening* program on New Year's Eve and *sang,* with a touch of Wilson Pickett in his voice, 'I'm going to wait 'til the midnight hour'?" Close to a thousand people in the World Theater, maybe hundreds of thousands listening, even in Alaska, ready to dance, at home? The same guy who's written personal essays for *All Things Considered* and read them with his voice at the edge of tears? He says he's afraid of *performing*? It may be that I do harbor some of the secret desires of the born entertainer, but that doesn't keep my hands from shaking.

Over the next couple of days I notice I'm staying close to the piano. Playing Hanon exercises, practicing the Vandall piece (I want to play it soon for our neighbors on their old Steinway grand), going back over the music I was trying to learn in the summer. And at work I'm often thinking about playing. It seems now I *want* to practice—there's nothing about it that I dread—and that's a big change.

We spend an hour wandering around a music store—

Foxes—in Falls Church, Virginia, and I bring home Alfred's Basic Adult Piano Course: lesson books for levels one, two, and three. I look ahead to the end of book three, to see how far this course would take you. Six pieces are included in an "Ambitious" section: "For those who would like to play well-known classics in their original form, and who are ambitious enough to apply a little extra effort to do so." The Bach Prelude in C Major is here; the "Trumpet Tune," by Jeremiah Clarke, which is often played as a wedding march; Chopin's Prelude in A Major; and Beethoven's *Moonlight* Sonata, the first movement. There would indeed be some work to it, but you could have a pretty impressive evening of music if you learned these pieces. Also at the store I found the Alfred edition of Schumann's *Scenes from Childhood,* op. 15. This is the book that has "Träumerei" on two pages instead of one. And I learn that "Träumerei" is the seventh in a series of thirteen short pieces, written at the same time; they are often played together in concert as a complete work. Foxes Music Company is a professional's store; at the cash register I'm asked if I'm a teacher. No, and as a matter of fact, I don't even *have* a teacher.

If I lived close enough to Vermont, I might sign up with Ned Phoenix. He charges twenty-five dollars an hour. He lives up on top of Wilkinson Mountain, outside the village—post office, library, Corner Store, Blue Dog Videos—of Townshend. A friend in Washington said, "Piano? You gotta go talk to Ned."

Wearing a wool cap and tan Carhartt coveralls, Ned Phoenix is waiting with his Toyota four-wheel-drive pickup. He looks a well-worn forty. "I'll meet you at the bottom of the hill; it gets rough from there," he told me on the phone. "Nine A.M.'s good. Let's do it in the daytime; I make my own electricity."

The truck takes us up slowly. "Let me clue you in as to what's going on. I've found my matching half. Her name's Wilma; she's nineteen; she came about a month ago and hasn't left." Ned explains that he moved to Wilkinson Mountain after his marriage broke up; he'd decided to clear the land and build a house by hand and make as strong a life as he could by himself.

Now Wilma sits on the bed, cutting out fabric squares for a quilt. A stove roars nearby, burning chunks of beech and maple. This large room, if the house were finished, would be the shop. For the present it's the only room that works. Ned carries water in from a spring; there's an outhouse near the trees in back. A tractor, a snowmobile, a small generator. Ned's grandfather was a piano tuner; his grandmother taught music into her nineties. His father is a retired tuner and cabinetmaker; his parents still live in Townshend. It was a musically dedicated home; four boys, they all played. Ned says his father would drive eight hours on Saturday to take him into Boston for lessons at the New England Conservatory of Music.

"I wanted to be a pipe organ man," Ned tells me. For

him the machinery became as intriguing as the music. He admired the nineteenth-century craftsmanship, loved the touch of brass and steel and ivory, the rush of wind through the tuned reeds. Organ rebuilding is his trade. Resurrection, he calls it. Somebody will buy a parlor organ at a farm auction someplace and dream of pumping the pedals and hearing the sweet, revenant tones of yesteryear; that person will end up with Ned Phoenix's phone number, and the organ goes on a truck to Vermont and up the mountain. Ned has the tools from a century ago and a cellarful of parts. "How do you find this stuff?" I wonder, and he says, "It finds me. After twenty-five years I'm known around the world. I don't mean it to sound egotistical, it's just that way." The work takes time, and Ned has arranged to have that available. "I just delivered an organ and got my entire yearly paycheck on one day. For once in my life I'm slightly ahead."

He shows me a collection of small organs made to fit on your lap; "rocking melodeons" they're called. Push down on one end, the bellows fills with air at the other. You play the melody on a row of small buttons. "They're just so neat," he says. "This was the popular music in America before the piano. Every home had one of these in 1850." And he takes a blanket off a large two-keyboard Victor Mustel reed organ. Made in Paris in 1903; Ned found it in Montreal. He plays a César Franck piece, written, he says, especially for the organ.

The air in the room jumps to life; the tones have a creamy whisper with a touch of mellow, throaty thunder.

But I've come for piano music, and so we finish the organ preamble and take a seat on the bench in front of Ned's old Fischer upright. It's one his dad found for him. It's actually a player piano, with the reproducing mechanics removed. Ned explains: "These old player pianos make fine instruments. They're solid, and the sound box is bigger—more volume." There's a glossy show business photograph on the music rack. It's a picture of "The Legendary Whitney Phoenix." Whitney, tuxedoed and smiling, is Ned's oldest brother. He plays year-round in Las Vegas, Ned says, cocktail lounge piano with classical overtones.

It is one note from a jazz alto saxophone player, though, that is at the very heart of Ned Phoenix's piano-teaching philosophy. "Ever hear Lee Konitz play?" he asks. "Do. You have to. I don't know how long he'll be around. The first note was worth all the big money I paid to hear him down in Brattleboro. It was just the most glorious sound. It's hot in the center and it just cooks and it emanates out, radiates out in all directions. There's no ending to the sound. It's just like looking at pictures of the sun; it just fades out.

"It's the tone; it's like Coltrane, you know," he says, turning to the piano. "You want to be inside the instrument, you want to be in here with these hammers hitting the strings." Ned's been working on a book based on his ideas about tone, and you can clearly *hear* why he's so passionate. He sits at the very edge of the piano bench, perched forward, his hands on a chord, and *leans* into the notes. The sound is produced from his body, not his fingers. He shows me how the finger chord sounds: plunky, percussive. And again the lean: warm, singing. "You don't tickle the ivories," he says, with scorn. "Instead of playing the tops of these ivory things you play the felt that's underneath."

And I try it. "Oh, sit back more, and sit up higher. Lean over so much that if you took your hands away, you'd do serious damage to your eyeglasses." I try a chord. "Don't push, lean." It sounds better. "You can lean fast and heavy," he says, to fill up the room with sound. "Or lean little, to make fireplace-size music.

"The piano is not an up-and-down instrument," Ned says. "If you play up and down all the time, that's a mistake. Music moves horizontally; every note goes to the next one. You play with your shoulders and arms and from your creative center—your pelvis area. How do you get the tone? You love the thing."

Ned Phoenix would not have many students here in rural Vermont. In the winter, when the road's bad, he meets them for lessons down in the valley at the high school. There is Brent, a young boy who's been blind from birth—a great student. He's learning "The Flight of the Bumblebee" from a tape Ned made for him. Another student, Liz, is blind also, the result of an accident. She's had trouble with pitch and carries around one of Ned's tuning forks. And Alan and Ben, father and son. They come to lessons together and go home to practice on an upright in their mud room. Ned says, "I treat the children like adults and I treat the adults like children." He's been known to offer scholarship lessons for those who can't pay, and every May he organizes a recital for all the students and anybody who'll show up to play anything. "People are banging on stuff who never hit anything in their life."

He wants the music to be simple. Sit at the piano. Narrow the vision. The fifty-two white keys, the thirty-six black ones become, with his teaching, just seven notes to learn. And since they belong together in a scale, they're easy to find and sound good, played one after the other, up and back down. Let's take the scale right in front of us: C major. "You know this song," he says, playing "Mary Had a Little Lamb." And he's right, how could you not find it on those seven white keys? "And look"—he shows me—"just play this chord with your other hand. Use your little finger, the middle finger, the thumb; you're playing the first, third, and fifth notes of the scale. Now move your hand up, and play the third, fifth, and seventh notes. That's another chord." I'm smiling as I play because he has taken me to a point of revelation, something that just hasn't registered in all the months before: You make the chords with the *odd numbers* in the scale!

So my right hand has the melody and I have two chords to play with the left and the idea is to change the chord when it feels right. We move on to "This Land Is Your Land," with three chords now, and it's only a little more difficult. Then quickly to the blues. The bass line rolls up out of the old piano. He plays "Frankie and Johnny," again easy to find in the right hand. And he shows me the three blues chords. Play each one two measures each and then switch according to a pattern that he first demonstrates, then writes down in my notebook. It's a twelve-bar blues, and the chord progression is so familiar that the new ones come chunking into their rightful places like bricks when you're building a wall. In two hours I could learn this. In time I could improvise around the chords.

"Let's go do some stove standing," Ned says. And we move to the room's warm side. He puts a kettle on the stove, opens a glass jar of dried peppermint, takes down three teacups and a jar of honey. Wilma smiles quietly.

So the learning's not all that hard, I say, but what about the piano? What do you tell people? "You can get a free one," he says. "Lots of those around. Just ask people, advertise, put up a notice. If you find one and it doesn't make any sound at all, don't take it, but usually you'll get something that works and you can spend a hundred fifty dollars or so to get it home and get one or two things fixed on it and tuned up. Play it for a couple of years; then push it off the porch." (I hold back from telling him that in Washington a family could spend most of that sort of piano budget in two hours at the Kennedy Center, paying $39.50 apiece for box seats to see, let's say, Alfred Brendel play Beethoven, plus the $6 for parking.)

"What if you want a good piano, though?" I ask. "How much should you spend?"

"Probably a thousand dollars," he says. "Get a big old upright. A Steinway, Chickering, Mason & Hamlin. Something solid." How do you know it's solid? Ask a piano guy to help you. Find someone like Ned's dad, who knows all the pianos within a hundred miles. Ned is a touch impatient with my questions. *Playing* is the important thing for him. Don't have a piano? Practice on the one at church, ask your neighbors, go to your grandmother's house.

On the drive back down through Vermont, I realize that we all make our choices in life. Ned Phoenix finds a way to have music in his. He wakes up on the top of Wilkinson Mountain and there's firewood to cut and organs to fix and students to teach. And long nights to play by candlelight. Denise Kahn, a teacher in New York City, also has days full of music, but a different sort of life entirely.

Go up Broadway past Lincoln Center on Saturday morning. The streets are full of students, old, arthritic women walking tiny, arthritic dogs. There's a blare of traffic and a bounce from the coffee bars, and you could go into Tower or HMV records and carry home boxed sets of Horowitz, Nat King Cole, Bill Evans—decades of listening in a snap of a credit card.

I did a story here at Juilliard, some years ago, about

the competitive spirit among students who were finishing degrees in piano performance. I repeated as apocryphal the "razor blade" legend: single-edge blades being inserted between the keys of practice room pianos; an unsuspecting fellow student would be cut and unable to perform. The people I interviewed all laughed about it but seemed to appreciate the idea that the story could have a bit of truth.

Denise Kahn's apartment is in a comfortable, calm building. "A lot of musicians live here. It feels very friendly."

We have coffee in her living room. It could be a scene in a New York movie: an impression of red, the oriental carpet, the chairs, shelves full of books, pale light through the windows, and the muted, floating traffic sounds. And the waiting tension of a piano: a Steinway A, built in 1896—"It belonged to my grandfather"—and rebuilt here in New York.

I won't be playing it; I've come only for a conversation. "She teaches adult beginners," a friend said. "She likes to."

Denise Kahn smiles. "It is such a fabulous intellectual challenge to teach someone to play the piano. You have no idea." She talks fast, expressively; you watch her hands. She is perhaps past forty, slim, dark hair.

I ask, "If someone calls you and wants to know what kind of progress can I expect in—?"

"I used to say five years." She laughs. "Now I say ten years. Oh, that's one of those questions that you're a fool if you try to answer. I've had people who couldn't get anywhere to save their lives, and I've had people in this apartment who have just blown my mind with what they've done. I teach a heart surgeon from New Jersey. Way the hell out, miles away. He'll come here after having been in the hospital all night, after having done three open-heart operations yesterday. He's been coming seven years; he does not miss a lesson. I taught him where middle C was; he's now playing Debussy preludes. He started in his forties. He has an insane, busy life, but he's got this laser-beam kind of understanding. To teach him, you have to appeal to his intelligence."

Then a strange story: "I had a business executive call me and say, 'I can only progress at the rate of an hour a week. I won't practice, I'll just come for the lesson.' And that's what he did, for ten years. I always thought he *would* break down and practice, but he didn't. He's gone now, transferred back to South Africa. He'd said he wanted to be able to play when he retired."

"How good did he get?" I wonder.

"He was okay, I guess. He could play the 'Maple Leaf Rag,' the original Scott Joplin version."

Denise leans forward on the couch. "And then there was the stockbroker who thought you could do it like a language-immersion course. He was thirty-five years old. He thought there was a special place in hell for people who did not realize their talent, and he wanted to play the piano. He was used to writing a check to solve his problems, so he paid me to sit with him for six hours a day every day and play the piano. We worked from January to June for six months. Five days a week. He was so intense; we didn't even go out for lunch. He would have sandwiches sent in. It was really grueling for me. But I learned something that was so interesting. He did not make much more progress than someone would who has only one lesson a week. It's just not something you can learn that way. There's a motor development that has to happen over time, and as hard as we worked, I was not able to get him to do that much more. It was a failure. It wasn't worth it."

Denise says the downside of teaching piano is that when someone has trouble learning, he or she inevitably has to blame her. Sometimes it ends badly. That hasn't happened often, but it's something she has recognized, and it's part of the reason she doesn't demand any certain amount of weekly practice from her students. "With adults you want to avoid a crash-and-burn situation. You don't want to give them a chance to get down on themselves." But most of the stories are happier: "I have a new guy. He's just had five lessons. He's so excited; he's always loved music. It was a revelation when I told him what an octave was, what a treble clef was. He said, 'These are terms I've heard all my life!' He comes here at eight o'clock in the morning before he goes to his law office, and he has his briefcase and his whole lawyer getup on, and he sits down at the piano like a little child."

At the first lesson Denise teaches a Bach prelude. She plays it first, then teaches it by rote, measure by measure, note by note; the left hand's easy, it's a repeating figure. "They can come in here knowing absolutely nothing and leave being able to play the first eight measures of the Bach C minor prelude. Each week I show them a few more measures, and after they've learned about a page of it—it's two pages long—I show them the music. Which looks quite hard; it has three flats. So I've reversed the whole process. First they learn what it sounds like and what it feels like; then they learn what it looks like. Their sight reading makes a quantum leap when they can put the symbols together with what they already know; all of a sudden the whole thing seems to click."

Denise shares with Ned Phoenix a concern that the students learn to play with their whole bodies, not just their fingers. "This is an exciting time in piano pedagogy. We have come out of two hundred years of the dark ages." And she goes to her piano to demonstrate. She begins "About Strange Lands and People," letting her shoulders and arms move in free, circular motions. It's a floating, melodic sound; this is one of the Schumann *Scenes from Childhood* pieces. "Piano technique came out of harpsichord technique, which is a terrible mistake. You really can play the harpsichord just by manufacturing energy with your fingers and cutting off all the muscles in your arms. But people bought that technique for the piano and played hours and hours of scales and exercises and were invested in it and passed it along to their students, who would spend thousands of hours playing that way. When I was a kid, it was 'Lift your fingers, strike the keys,' with no wisdom beyond that. I studied with some very famous teachers, and they'd say, 'Hold all your fingers down and trill like this for an hour.' The aim was to strengthen the small muscles of the fingers and . . . *it's cuckoo*. It's damaging; I had terrible tendinitis. Once you understand that you can avoid the percussive effect on the fingers, that the arm is really supplying the motion, it's like being let out of *jail*. You make larger, continuous motions behind a group of notes, and so you overcome this inherent problem of the piano, which is that the keys go up and down but the music goes horizontally. It's very exciting to realize that, and you can hear it; the beauty of the piano is in the flow."

She plays the Schumann with free movement and then with fingers only. The difference is dramatic. Many pianists *do* play with an intuitive physical sense, she says: "They fall out of the womb playing naturally." But the students who play *without* feeling and tone are being taught that way. "The Russian students," she says, "who are coming over here now in droves have had very strict training. It's all fingers and it's tight and you can really hear it. It doesn't sound musical. It sounds too notey."

Denise is fond of organizing chamber music sessions in her apartment. She'll ask—or hire—a violinist, a cellist to come in and play with some of her piano students. "There is something about the performance situation that is very special. There are things inside you that you just can't get to except under extraordinary circumstances." She agrees it's also very scary. "My heart surgeon student has played in some of my sessions, and he says it's the hardest thing he's ever done in his life. He went to medical school, and he does surgery, but this is terrifying." She adds, "When you play with others, you have the responsibility to keep going no matter what, and you have to transcend yourself; it's like someone's holding a gun to your head.

"Do you know about Inderal?" she asks, speaking of the beta-blocker drug. "It's actually great stuff. I use it in high-pressure situations and recommend it to students when they get very nervous. I take five milligrams. Once years ago, when I was a neophyte, I hadn't practiced enough for a performance, so I made up for it by taking more Inderal. Eighty milligrams or something ridiculous. And what happens is you lose your will; you have no adrenaline at all: I didn't want to put my hands on the keyboard. It's the great unspoken thing nobody talks about; everyone I know takes it, people whose names I won't tell you because they asked me not to. There's a stigma in the music world. People think it's like taking steroids, but it simply blocks the flow of adrenaline that gives you the physical manifestation of nerves. And why not? You can play wonderfully, you have great technique, and suddenly you're stricken with this horrible ailment. Life is not perfect."

Denise has been reacquainting herself with what it's like to be a student. She's started learning cello, taking two lessons a week. She loves the instrument as well as the chance to learn more about the student-teacher relationship. "As an adult you miss that sort of thing, a regular meeting with someone who's helping you with some aspect of yourself and you feel very nurtured and cared about. You pay some shrink to listen to you every week, is what most people do. This week my cello teacher canceled a lesson, and I was upset about it. It's a very intensely personal thing to study an instrument, and since adults are emotionally more rich and more mature, the nature of the relationship with a teacher tends to be that way as well. I'm so completely involved; it just takes you out of your life."

Denise emphasizes that learning an instrument, a skill, is different from learning by reading a book, and it's the kind of learning that adults usually no longer experience. "Music is such a living thing. I think you learn so much about yourself sitting at the keyboard, and I'm constantly learning just by teaching."

The conversation is quieter now, slower. "It's about integrity. Even at a stupid level like letting yourself get away with a wrong fingering and knowing perfectly well you've put the wrong finger on that note and not doing anything about it. That is a lack of integrity as much as glossing over stuff at the highest levels. Your ego is constantly being teased when you play, and if you're really going to meet a Beethoven sonata head-on, it's not about you, it's not about how good you are or how fast you can play; it's really about getting beyond yourself."

Denise is still, and then says, "I'm sorry, I'm feeling very emotional today. A very close friend of mine is dying, and talking about music makes me connect with her. And I was with her last night . . ."

After a pause she continues: "Coming with humility to a piece of music—it's contacting the best parts of yourself. The part that feels deeply, and you have to be willing to have those feelings; a lot of people aren't. Feelings have been so cheapened."

"What do you suppose that's about, really, the way music can be so emotional?" I ask.

Denise says, "Music can create these beautiful moments out of nothing. We can be sitting here and play a phrase and suddenly there's beauty. Anyone who relates to music knows that feeling of being touched by a piece so deeply—and God, that's such a privilege."

Moments go by, softly.

I ask, "Do you know the scene from the movie *Five Easy Pieces*?"

Denise laughs and answers in an instant, "Where he plays the Chopin E minor prelude?" Jack Nicholson—a musical family's wayward, cynical son—is playing the piano for Susan Anspach. She's attracted to him; the camera swirls; she grows misty-eyed. He stops. She says, "That was beautiful; I'm surprised. I was really very moved." Nicholson laughs. "I picked the easiest piece I can think of. I first played it when I was eight years old, and I played it better then." Anspach answers, "Can't you understand it was the feeling I was affected by?" Jack Nicholson says, "I faked a little Chopin, you faked a big response."

Back home in Washington, November's symbolic ending arrives. Thanksgiving is a grand day for us at NPR. It's a holiday I like to work because the *All Things Considered* staff puts together a memorable potluck dinner; we've been doing it for about fifteen years. It was started so the single people, especially, would be sure to have a Thanksgiving meal. Neenah and I get up early to cook a turkey, and she brings it in at noon. Also on the table: baked ham, cheese grits, homemade breads, sweet potato pie. We are hoping for an unexciting news day around the world, so we can pay proper attention to the food.

And some musician friends stopped in a couple of days before Thanksgiving, on their way to their homes for the holiday. I taped an interview in our music studio with Anne Hills, from Bethlehem, Pennsylvania, and Cindy Mangsen and Steve Gillette, who live in Bennington, Vermont. They sat around with guitars, and a concertina, singing a few songs and talking about music and family gatherings in the past. Anne and Cindy have a new recording of duets, and I'm quite taken with the way they sing "Never Grow Old," the title song. It's an old, dignified hymn that is at once sad and reassuring:

"I have heard of a land/on a faraway strand/'tis a beautiful home of the soul." And in the mail two weeks later I receive the music for the hymn, written out by hand, for piano. I take it home, and yes, I can play it.

DECEMBER

My wife falls in love with a piano player in a tuxedo, and the night is still young

WE SPEND A SATURDAY AFTERNOON CLEANING OUT THE GA-rage, creating a pile of trash for pickup at the curb: scraps of wood and foam rubber and screen wire, plastic flower pots, an old TV stand. We'll have room now for Neenah's boat.

At sundown on Sunday night, in an empty house, I play "Träumerei" all the way through for the first time; I'm trying to learn it secretly, to surprise Neenah at Christmas. I'm planning to put on my old tuxedo and light some candles and really have a show.

It takes a long time to figure out the rest of the notes; it's only two pages of music. Vladimir Horowitz plays it at two minutes, thirty-two seconds; my version would run closer to twenty minutes. I hold my breath, I've noticed, looking for notes. But I am reassured each time I play the B-flat grace note in the left hand; it appears in the third measure. The same phrase comes along later in the piece, with the B-flat beginning a climb to the finish. This single note has the feeling of the whole composition for me.

Neenah has gone grocery shopping, taking along Šejla, our Sarajevo friend. They've been getting together once a week or so. Šejla loves the supermarket, likes to push the cart, enjoys trying to puzzle out in English the names of the cheeses and all the different kinds of fish. For someone whose family is in Bosnia, a shelf of cereals in an American supermarket must be a melancholy sight.

I have only an hour at the piano before they come back to put the groceries away and fix dinner. There will be another fifteen minutes later in the evening, when Neenah drives Šejla back to the house where she's staying. This sneaking around to find time at the piano reminds me of when I was trying to quit smoking. Neenah would say, "You coming with me?" "No, that's okay, I'll just stay here and finish this book. You have fun." And I'd have a cigarette lit before the car cleared the driveway. It looks doubtful that I can finish "Träumerei" by Christmas. I really need a teacher's help, but I wouldn't be able to get away for lessons. I just don't think I can make much progress running into the office to play a few notes while Neenah takes the dogs out before bedtime. It would be easier, I think, to have an affair than to learn this little piece of music.

My twin brother calls tonight from Los Angeles. I rarely hear from him, but he's been talking to our mother in Ohio and he's worried. She seems a bit downhearted, having problems with dizziness and not getting much help or reassurance from a new specialist she's seen in Cincinnati. I call to talk with her for a while, but it's hard to tell much at this distance. She does sound fragile. She's taking a new medication for her dizziness, but it won't start working for another two weeks. I wish now Neenah and I had gone to Ohio for the Thanksgiving weekend; Mom says they didn't have a big dinner; she didn't feel like cooking. I promise we'll be there—yes, with both dogs—at Christmastime. And could we find a piano so I could play something for you? "Oh, sure," she says, "we'll have a recital." Now I'll have to learn a couple of Christmas carols, in addition to "Träumerei."

"If the devil came and said you could make a deal?" I asked Neenah one evening when we were out to dinner. "You could be *one* kind of piano player; you'd be *fantastic* but only in one style of music. Who would you want to play like?" She hates questions like this, but I insisted.

"George Gershwin," she said. It was a really fine answer, and then *I* had to figure out what to say.

"Jerry Lee Lewis," I joked, and told her the story about being a teenager and hearing "Whole Lot of

Shakin' Going On" for the first time in the teen center
in Kentucky. It seemed the right choice for a barbecue
place lit by blue neon, especially when that very song
came over the speakers only ten minutes later. But my
true favorite pick-only-one pianist would be Butch
Thompson. No band, no trio, just Butch Thompson's
blues and stride and jazz and touches of Joplin and Jelly
Roll Morton and Eubie Blake. One tune in particular
I'd like to play: "How Long Blues." I have it on a CD
called *Chicago Breakdown.* It's slow, and you get the
feeling the studio was dark and Butch got there before
anyone else and slipped his coat off to see how the piano
was sounding, remembering the opening notes to "How
Long Blues" and then just going on through to an end.

A mid-December travel thought begins to form:
Butch lives in St. Paul, and I have another Twin Cities'
story idea that I've been saving for *All Things Considered.* A pianist named Lorie Line. I talk with Ellen
Weiss, my boss: "People I trust in Minnesota are telling
me about this pianist who started playing part-time in
Dayton's department store and now is selling a million
dollars' worth of CDs and is selling out Orchestra Hall
in Minneapolis. I kind of see it as a business story."

"Go," she says. "I'll send up an engineer from Chicago to meet you."

Lorie Line answers the doorbell at noon. She is very
small, very happy, and possibly very tired; she flew in
this morning from Omaha, the last of a ten-city tour.
We sit at her living-room piano, a Kawai grand. Rick

Karr has a microphone near the piano's sounding board; I'm holding another mike for the conversation. And the Lorie Line story unfolds:

MS. LINE: Even as a six-year-old I thought, *This is great. This is what I want to do.*

NDA: Was the purchase of a piano a big thing for your parents, financially?

MS. LINE: Yeah. It was five or six hundred dollars. It was a big purchase for them back in those days. We lived in Reno, and they went to Sacramento to get the piano, to pick it out. And I remember sitting on the curb on my birthday, waiting for that piano to come. And I sat without my shoes, and there was water just going down the curb, people watering their lawns, and all of a sudden here comes this big truck with the piano on it. My parents made me promise that I would play until I was eighteen years old.

NDA: Then when is the moment when you were sure that you were a piano player?

MS. LINE: I was nine. I had entered a competition in Reno. It was a competition for twelve-year-olds. I got up and I played and I won. I remember sitting up there, playing my best and feeling like I had played very well. And getting down and having the judges look at me and talk to me, and I felt special.

NDA: Did you think you were going to be a concert pianist?

MS. LINE: I knew I would perform. I just didn't know

how I would get there. I never wanted to read and memorize. I didn't want to play in a pit. I didn't want to practice all day by myself. I knew that someday I would be able to do this, but it would have been just for smaller crowds or in a department store.

NDA: But you don't mean that when you were twelve or thirteen, you were thinking, *Well, when I get to be twenty-five, at least I'll be playing in a department store?*

MS. LINE: No, you don't have the aspiration of growing up and playing in the department store, that's for sure. In fact, it's very humbling to sit down and do that, and watch all these people with business suits on in their lunch hour rush by and have them say to their friend, "She should get a real job."

NDA: You were working for a construction company here in the Twin Cities. And the Dayton's job was part-time, weekends, nights. Why did you decide to do that?

MS. LINE: I went to work from six to nine every night and twelve to five on the weekends. My husband and I had been in Dayton's and had walked past a pianist, and he said to me, "You really should be playing. Here you are working as director of marketing for a construction company, but your gift is music." I thought it was a great idea. I auditioned; I got the job. And I kept my other job during the day, and I thought if anyone I know from that world sees me here playing the piano, I'll just say I'm trying it out,

or I'm just filling in part-time. But after five months
the response was so overwhelming. It changed my life
in five months, and there was no way I could stay
with my day job.

NDA: What do you mean, people were coming up to the
piano and talking to you about their response, about
the way they felt about your music?

MS. LINE: They would come up to the piano and say,
"This is what I am looking for, this particular style of
music. And there isn't anybody who is doing this.
There isn't even actually a radio station that is fulfill-
ing my needs for music the way you can do this. Do
you have an album out? Do you have a tape out?"
And I thought, *Aha, this is why I've been in business so
long*—I've been in marketing ten years. "Let me take
your name and number and address, and if I ever do
anything, I'll be sure to let you know." After just a
few months I knew that I could recoup at least the
money I'd put out making an album from the people
who had stopped by.

NDA: Now can you explain in musical terms what it was
that person heard in your music that she wasn't hearing someplace else?

MS. LINE: I have a real strong melody line. I learned this
in my classical training, to keep the melody on the
top and how to make a melody line sing, and then I
know how to support it with the right selection of the
notes underneath to create a flow that is appealing to
the ear.

I ask Lorie Line for an example of how she would change a song to put it into her style. "Yeah," she says, "let's play Bob Dylan's 'Blowin' in the Wind.' " She plays it the regular way, quite straight. Sounds fine but dull. "Okay, here's how I would do it." And the song's melody begins to flow; it drifts and dances above the bass line, which also is now in motion. "I do a lot with arpeggios," Lorie says, and that is pure understatement. Her music *is* arpeggios, the notes of the chord played separately rather than together, starting with the lowest tone; it's a pleasant, open sound.

And she picks songs that people have heard before and probably like: "A Whole New World," the theme from *Aladdin*, Eric Clapton's "Tears in Heaven," "Ashokan Farewell." She plays a bit of classical, some hymns, Christmas tunes, some songs she's written as well. New CDs and tapes every year, plus sheet music, concert ticket sales. I learn that I had undersold this story to my producer when I mentioned that Lorie Line was doing a million dollars' worth of business. That was last year's figure. This year it's two million.

We drive to the offices of Time Line Productions, for some shoptalk. Tonight's concert piano will be a Yamaha, a switch from Steinway. Lorie says the action is easier on the Yamaha. "The tinkly, high fast notes—I just can't play them as well on a Steinway." She's played Steinway pianos for ten straight nights now; her hands are tired, and she has adhesive tape on several of her fingertips where the skin is splitting. Her staff is busy packing up

CDs and tapes for Orchestra Hall; they expect to sell ten thousand dollars' worth tonight. Lorie Line's music is now in Musicland stores and Sam Goody's, but most of the sales are at the concerts or to people on the mailing list; the original Dayton's list of five hundred names now is securely inside the Time Line computer and has just passed fifteen thousand. Her products are also carried by gift shops around the country. People walk in the stores; the music is playing; they go up to the counter and buy the tape. Lorie says, "It wasn't the major retailers that started this whole thing. It was me taking it to these small little tiny shops and then all these people coming in and hearing it and saying this is exactly my kind of music. And then they have guests over for dinner, and those people go find the music."

Lorie and Tim Line, her husband, who's running the company, also laugh at the idea of signing up with a major record label. They're selling the CDs by mail for sixteen dollars, and it's their profit. With a record company all they'd earn is a royalty. And a big company wouldn't understand Lorie's market. Lorie and Tim know that they're selling to people who like music but don't usually buy it, who'll walk out of record stores because the clerks are all twenty years old.

At Orchestra Hall, before the concert, I have a talk with Tim. It isn't much of a real conversation. Tim is practiced at delivering an image that Minnesotans can identify with and cheer for: a young mother who was selling concrete parking structures for a construction company and playing piano at Dayton's on the weekend and now she's playing at Orchestra Hall for two thousand people. He does seem quite sincere about their goals: to sell a million copies of a recording someday and to be able to sell out Christmas concerts in twenty cities. Perhaps even New York. "Carnegie Hall?"

He laughs. "Sure. I wonder how much it costs to rent it."

Tim goes off, busy before curtain time. He's the promoter tonight. Their company hires the halls, does the advertising, sells the tickets, and keeps the profits.

It's a Christmas program, with Lorie Line and her Pop Chamber Orchestra. She's onstage with nine other musicians; they open loudly with Vivaldi's *The Four Seasons*. Lorie looks sleek and sparkly, short dark hair, short black Donna Karan dress (my fashion information comes from the *Wall Street Journal* a few days later; it also has a reporter here, and she's got the inside information on the dress). "The Holly and the Ivy" and "The Little Drummer Boy" follow in busy arrangements. Lorie writes the music for all the instruments, working in her office on a Yamaha Clavinova. On the electronic keyboard she plays the trumpet leads, the cello harmonies, building up the song part by part, and the completed music is notated on the computer screen, then printed for the musicians.

After each song Lorie gets up from the piano and walks to a microphone at front center stage, where she talks to the audience about the music and the other players. Liberace, the grandest of contemporary piano performers, used to do the same thing, even on his television shows; he'd leave the piano and talk to the viewers. When we spoke at her home, I had asked Lorie about Liberace. She said, "Yeah, I saw him play as a kid maybe three or four times, and as a freshman in college I dated his drummer, so I got to see him a couple of times then. I was even motivated by him because he would take requests from the audience; I do that now myself."

And it's a popular part of the Lorie Line show—request time. She'll play a medley: What would people like to hear? The audience starts yelling out song titles: "Stairway to Heaven" (big laughs), "Piano Man," "Beauty and the Beast," Pachelbel's "Canon," "Amazing Grace," "Moon River"—and "Rocket Man." For the request medley she sits alone onstage, and you can finally appreciate just how good a piano player she is. She's quickly arranged—in her mind—about fifteen songs, and they flow and spin and change keys and make sense together.

After the concert I talk with some of her fans, who are glowing. One says, "She can touch the piano and just can make you cry, it's just so gorgeous." And there's a backstage reception, with food and drinks. Tim Line had set aside 125 comp tickets for tonight's show: for friends and media and important locals; usually it means the people who can most easily afford tickets will get in free. Lorie is leaning against a railing, exhausted, trying to smile for everyone. And I talk with Peter Ostroushko; he's become an old Minnesota friend by now. Peter's playing mandolin and fiddle in Lorie Line's Pop Orchestra; he's been traveling with her at Christmas for several years. That does not stop him from being a little perturbed at her success. "Hell, yes, I'm resentful. And I'm jealous," he says, then smiles. He likes Lorie and admires her energy. "She knows how to market her music. I wasn't trained to do that. I slung hamburgers when I was in high school. I was a dishwasher. I cleaned inhalation therapy equipment at General Hospital, and most of the time I played music, that's what I did."

Lorie Line had told me earlier, "There are a lot of people out there who are musicians—gifted and talented —that are in this alternative area. And they're playing what they really like. But nobody else likes it." Perhaps it's more accurate to say not enough people like it. I've seen Peter Ostroushko play at Georgetown University in Washington on a night when he could make your heart drop with his fiddle music, when the emotions of the entire audience would rise and follow a phrase as if everyone in the room were playing the instrument.

The next morning, close to eleven, I find Butch Thompson's house on an older street in St. Paul. "There's a tree out front with Christmas lights on it; I'll turn it on," he said on the phone, giving directions. It's a familiar, dry, humorous voice. He sounds the same on the phone as he always did on *A Prairie Home Companion.*

Part of the genius of Garrison Keillor's program from the World Theater ("in downtown St. Paul") was its organic *quietness*. A writer good enough to have published humor in the *New Yorker*, and musicians—among them Peter Ostroushko and Butch Thompson—good enough to play anywhere, sort of getting together on a Saturday evening to fool around with songs and pretend stories from Lake Wobegone. It sounded, to a listener, just like the guys from the neighborhood.

We sit at the dining-room table, having coffee. Butch is wearing moccasin slippers and brown corduroy pants, a dark blue shirt. He has elegant gray hair and a long mustache; he could have been a jazz player back in the thirties, walking into a club wearing a fedora and a tailored cashmere topcoat, with his clarinet case under his arm.

He's from a very small town up on the St. Croix River, about an hour's drive from St. Paul—a few streets of white frame houses, a general store. The upright piano in the living room, when he was growing up, was painted lavender; Butch doesn't recall why. His mother liked to play, and he remembers that every time she sat down at the piano the piece she would always play first was "Träumerei."

"After I got big enough to reach the keys—I guess I was five or so—I couldn't stay away from it. I was looking for *consonant* sounds, and I know I was fascinated when I discovered the octave; I really liked the way those two notes sounded together."

There was, Butch says, in his town of Marine on St. Croix, the proverbial blind tuner, who would come by and show him how to find a few things on the keyboard. There was a John Thompson instruction book in the piano bench. And a woman, one of the neighbors, who knew quite a bit of music and agreed to teach a few lessons. Butch became her first student. He was six years old then.

"Dad played those old records loud. And I liked them too; it was the one thing that really connected us." Butch's father was a truck driver, running long distances. And he collected music from the 1940s: Teddy Wilson's piano tunes, Tommy Dorsey's orchestra—all of it reissued on 45s. Butch also liked boogie-woogie and blues and later Fats Domino and Jerry Lee Lewis. "I would try to get my father to listen to 'Whole Lot of Shakin' Going On.' And I tried to convince him about Elvis; I was a big Elvis fan. He did like, my dad, to hear Elvis sing 'Peace in the Valley.' "

Butch also learned clarinet in high school, and he formed a little band that would play for twist contests at the dances. He went on to study piano and music theory at the University of Minnesota, but he was starting to drift backward in time. "I knew I wasn't going to be a modernist. I was attracted to the visceral side of jazz. I never really liked the cooler side of playing. I wanted things to be more direct. In college I started playing clarinet with the Hall Brothers New Orleans Jazz Band; we were doing a lot of Jelly Roll Morton tunes. In July

1962 we went down to New Orleans and played for a party at Preservation Hall—the kind of thing where people would put fifty cents in a coffee can to pay the musicians for a Sunday afternoon's work. And we were in town for a while and I got to hear George Lewis play. Clarinet. He was sixty-one that summer, and he was *past* being a legend. I was absolutely knocked out by his playing; he absolutely killed me. There was so much emotion and power in his playing, and it just opened up the whole culture of the older New Orleans musicians for me. I was ready for something."

Butch enjoyed playing clarinet as well, but despite the inspiration, he stayed with the piano as his more natural instrument. He listened to Louis Armstrong's trumpet. He admired a "certain sonority" in the way Ray Charles played chords. He mentions Eubie Blake, Nat Cole, Jimmy Yancey as influential, and especially Jelly Roll Morton: "His playing has sort of a ringing quality to it, and a very distinctive rhythmic content. Rhythm is its own kind of virtuosity. For a time I wanted to play just like him, and I'd play the old records over and over again, transcribing the notes, trying to figure out details; on the older records you can't tell exactly what the notes are. How does he voice those chords? It's hard to know. It's so frustrating that Jelly Roll Morton was never filmed playing the piano; then I'd have a better chance. Finally, though, I said to myself, 'You can't actually *be* this other person,' and I knew I had to find my own way back into this music."

It's lunchtime, and Mary Ellen, Butch's wife, joins us; she's made some chili, and we have a salad. We talk some about last night's Lorie Line concert at Orchestra Hall; they've been hearing a lot about her music but haven't seen her play. "Sold out, really!" they say. Mary Ellen takes care of Butch's mailing list; she says the response is really pretty good, you can sell quite a few albums by direct mail. And it's a way to keep people informed about Butch's college appearances and community concerts. Butch just smiles when I tell them that Lorie Line's list has now passed fifteen thousand.

We walk to the piano in the living room—a Kawai grand he bought used from a woman in town. Butch plays a few chords. I've asked him about technique; what's difficult for him now? Rhythm things sometimes, he says; sometimes you can't have the right swing feeling. He adds: "Only in the last ten years do I feel like I'm getting close to what I want. What's hard is to have a distinctive touch. When I hear Teddy Wilson, Earl Hines, Rubinstein, Horowitz, I recognize that personal sound instantly. It's how the piano sounds under your fingers."

Butch is playing in town tonight, over in Minneapolis at a music café. He has a new CD called *Yulestride*, so it's a holiday affair. The room fills up fast; I find a stool at the bar. A black Yamaha piano waits onstage, under purple and green and red spotlights. People at the tables are eating and talking. At seven o'clock Butch comes out. He's wearing a blue suit, double-breasted, with a red bow tie. He carries a glass mug of coffee. He sits, nods at the audience, and begins "It Came upon a Midnight Clear." Slow ripples of familiar notes at first, then a tempo change into a fast stride arrangement, the left hand bouncing across the lower octaves, then thundering up the scale and back down, the right hand racing with the melody. "The fast music is the easiest," he told me. "When I go out to play, I'll often start with something fast just to get it out of the way, so the audience can say, 'Oh, okay, he's good. Now we'll listen.'"

But tonight—mostly—they don't. People are still standing around as if it were a cocktail party, and they're talking at the tables as well, looking up to notice that Butch has finished a tune and applauding to be polite. Butch starts playing again, and the bartender wants to tell me about a local microbrewery beer and how they have great tours on the weekend. Butch plays a sad version of "God Rest Ye Merry Gentlemen," and I watch women who all have the same hairstyle marching off to the bathroom. His "O Little Town of Bethlehem" is a jazzy blues, and I hear a waiter explaining that they can't serve cappuccino while the music's playing because of the noise the machine makes frothing the milk—espresso's fine, though. He plays an uptempo "Jingle Bells," and a couple goes out on the floor to dance. But a man and his wife who told me they'd driven all the way in from South Dakota to see Butch Thompson play move their chairs far over to the edge of the bandstand, as close to the piano as possible, so they can have a chance of hearing just music. Butch seems okay with all this; he's played in a few bars before. He finishes "I'll Be Home for Christmas" and then tells a piano player's story: Chicago in the late 1930s. Fats Waller, Duke Ellington, Billy Kyle, Count Basie all together in Waller's hotel room after their respective gigs. It's Christmas Eve, and they can't go home. Fats plays the portable organ he travels with, and they all sing Christmas carols. One of them said later, "That was the weepingest bunch of cats you ever did see."

Near the close of his set Butch plays the Fats Waller tune "Chelsea." The lights sparkle off the ends of the moving keys. There's a great tension in the music—slow chords that sound like bells. This is the moment, I know, when the devil could ease up next to me and make the deal.

The Christmas weekend finally arrives. I've been apprehensive. I'd need several more months' practice before I could play "Träumerei," but I'll push on with the plan. Anyway, it's about the only present I'll have for Neenah.

Christmas Day is coming up on Sunday, and on Friday I take the day off work. Early tomorrow morning we'll put both dogs in the car and drive out to southern Ohio, where my mother and stepfather live in a retirement community. "You're bringing the dogs, aren't you?" Mom always asks. And I've promised to play the piano, but there's been some confusion. My mother called the community center in the village to ask if we could come and use the grand piano there, but the activity director misunderstood and started getting ready for a concert; perhaps a hundred people would love to hear someone's son from out of town play the piano. We had to beg off, explaining I was only a beginner. Instead, Mom has found a piano at a friend's house, a couple who'll be away this weekend.

I've practiced "Away in a Manger," from a Christmas carol book, and a simple Alfred arrangement of "The Entertainer" and I'll play the Vandall prelude that I learned in Vermont. My mother will expect some boogie-woogie, though. One of her favorite old photographs is one she took during what she calls my "James Dean" period.* In this snapshot I'm maybe thirteen years old. Wearing a white shirt, Ray-Ban sunglasses, a sort of blond ducktail haircut, and an expression on my face that is close to arrogance. I cannot recall ever feeling that way. (I did assume, though, I remember, that I was somehow going to have a reckless life.) There is also the chance, in Ohio, that I'll play "Träumerei."

Neenah and I go out for lunch and some shopping. She finds a small blue Swiss Army knife, and a tiny flashlight, to go into a Christmas stocking for Šejla. I stop by the hardware store for bags of salt; last winter it was terribly icy. And I wander through a computer store, watching bewildered men trying, at the last minute, to learn what CD-ROM technology is all about.

* See the author photo on this book's flap.

At home we bring in some firewood, start cooking supper; Šejla's coming over later. The tree's up and decorated; Neenah starts getting the gifts together. I go out for about a three-mile run in the cold air, just before sunset. The running helps. What's the problem here? I ask myself. It's just some piano piece, and it's a *present;* who cares how well you play it?

I get into a hot bath. Neenah's in the next room, wrapping presents, listening to *All Things Considered.* In the tub I play through the music in my mind and think over the strategy. This should be a quick *shock,* I decide. I dry off, run into the bedroom, put on the white dress shirt and find the cuff links and studs and bow tie and dance into the pants and don't worry about which way the cummerbund goes and squeeze into the black shoes and put on the tuxedo jacket and—smile at the mirror! This might work. At least she didn't catch me halfway dressed.

I find a candle, the brass candlestick, matches, and walk into the room where Neenah's sitting on the floor with the ribbons and wrapping paper and watch her eyes grow wide. "What?" she asks, grinning.

I say, "I'll just turn off this radio for you. And light this candle for us." She stands up, blinking. I place a chair just to the right of the piano bench. I place Neenah on the chair. I sit on the bench. The Steinway 1098 is black, the white keys shiny. I'm in black and white. The candle flame dances with light . . . the world becomes small. And I play.

It gets hard to breathe and pay attention to the notes coming up. There's my lovely B-flat and then the five notes with the right hand leading up to the F—and I play it with some confidence. Then the second melody phrase, and the repeat comes. My hands seem okay, but my right foot is shaking on the sustain pedal, and I can't figure out how to stop it. The difficult part comes up, and I play very slowly, holding the pedal down so that the next note, when I find it, will sound connected. The music begins to sound hushed, eloquent; even the wrong notes seem to have a special quality. I can barely see Neenah, off to my right; I would dare not turn to look. And I move from the messed-up middle section to the final measures, the melody returning, the B-flat, the F, then a grand and difficult chord, just before the end. I play the chord, and I know Neenah is crying. What surprises me is that I'm crying too.

Afterword

Sɪᴛ ᴅᴏᴡɴ ɴᴇxᴛ ᴛᴏ ᴍᴇ ʜᴇʀᴇ ᴏɴ ᴛʜᴇ ᴘɪᴀɴᴏ ʙᴇɴᴄʜ, ᴀɴᴅ ᴡᴇ can play a little "Heart and Soul" together and talk a bit. I'll take this bouncing left-hand rhythm part, and you can come in on the melody. Just one finger, that's all. When we get to the end, we'll go back to the top and keep it going.

This is my kind of piano playing. Sounds good and it's fun and it is *real.* Someone once analyzed a recording of Schumann's C Major Toccata, op. 7, and found the piece was played at an average speed (including the chords) of 24.1 notes a *second.* That's nothing but a comet flashing across the night sky.

I've spent an unplanned year with the piano. And

while I'm happy with the way it all ended, I'd change a few things if I could, life being easier lived backward. You might ask, "Did you really have to buy that piano?" A fair question: Why do you have to spend eleven thousand dollars? The answer is: I did, but you don't. There's no regret of my purchase. The Steinway 1098 upright has settled down nicely after its humidity troubles (I did install the dehumidifier device), and it's pleasing to play. Also, buying the piano was an impulsive, absolute, drastic action; I had no choice but then at least to try to play. But I think it makes more sense to rent a piano for a year or so. You begin to learn the way the instrument sounds and what size piano seems right for you and your home (and you could be on the lookout for a great used piano deal in the meantime). Another question: "What about the electronic keyboards?" They solve problems of space, don't need tuning, don't suffer in damp or dry air. At the beginning I was sure I would find a keyboard that I would like, but it never happened. I played lots of them in music stores, and I even borrowed a Kurzweil PC88, regarded as a "pianist-friendly high-end" instrument (two thousand dollars plus). I admire the versatility of keyboards, and certainly if I were sixteen and wanted a way into *music,* I'd have to have one, but I don't like the touch and the sound of the notes. I'm just looking for a way into the *piano.*

And as we play along with "Heart and Soul," you surely will ask, "What about that computer course anyway, and shouldn't you have been taking lessons from a real teacher?" Well, maybe, and yes, I would answer. I had some good times learning the notes and how to play chords, watching it all on the computer screen, but the second time around I'd probably skip the extra expense and just start with the first Alfred book for beginning adults. And I would take lessons. Perhaps not so often, though; once every three or four weeks seems right for me. (I wonder, as you must, what would have happened if I had met a teacher like Denise Kahn back in February.)

"And that play-by-ear course? Is that any good?" you wonder. I've got the David Sudnow tapes on a shelf, and I'll try them again soon. Even better would be to take his course in person. I probably was a year or two ahead of myself, thinking I could learn jazz piano by ear, but I do think it's a solid concept. A question that may not occur is: "What sort of *listening* are you doing?" When I talked with Butch Thompson in St. Paul, I asked what he would want to know about someone who would approach him for lessons. "I'd ask right away how much listening time that person had." And it rings true that hearing great piano playing keeps you going as a beginner (my favorite at the moment is Earl ["Fatha"] Hines). And I think it's important to find the right *music* to *play*. "Träumerei" worked well for me. And I keep in mind Albert Einstein's story. He took violin lessons from age six to fourteen, but he really began to learn only after he became entranced by Mozart's sonatas. Einstein said later that he believed love is a better teacher than a sense of duty.

The last question—and the best one—is "Why do it at all? Why throw the piano into the mix of stuff you're already not getting done?" The answer can be found in the conversation with Denise Kahn, back in November. In fact, Steve Ross, my editor at Delacorte, phoned from New York when he read this chapter and said, "I think I have a title for you. It's in the text: 'And Suddenly There's Beauty.'" We eventually decided the phrase would be a bit obscure to be a good title, but it remains the soul of the book and the truth of my experience. Denise Kahn, talking quietly in her apartment, said, "We can be sitting here and play a phrase and suddenly there's beauty."

I'll just scoot off the piano bench now and let you start playing by yourself.

References and Reading

IF THERE IS TO BE A PIANO IN YOUR FUTURE, THE SINGLE indispensable reference is *The Piano Book: Buying & Owning a New or Used Piano*, by Larry Fine (Brookside Press, Jamaica Plain, Mass.). You'll want the third edition (green cover).

For history I've enjoyed Arthur Loesser's *Men, Women, and Pianos: A Social History* (Dover Publications, New York); Harold Schonberg's *The Great Pianists* (Simon and Schuster); *A Left Hand like God: A History of Boogie-Woogie Piano*, by Peter Silvester (Da Capo, New York); *The Steinway Saga: An American Dynasty*, by D. W. Fostle (Scribner); *Robert Schumann: His Life and Works*, by Ronald Taylor (Universe Books, New York).

For jazz inspiration, *American Musicians*, by Whitney Balliett (Oxford). For classical, Otto Friedrich's *Glenn Gould: A Life and Variations* (Vintage). For fun, *A Left Hand like God: A History of Boogie-Woogie Piano*.

Charles Cooke's *Playing the Piano for Pleasure* (Greenwood Press, Westport, Conn., 1941) stands alone as an account of an amateur's devotion. You would count it as a treasure if you found an older copy in a used-book store.

All these books as well as others I've mentioned in the text have been invaluable for my research and writing. For a comprehensive listing of about a thousand works see *The Pianist's Reference Guide: A Bibliographical Survey*, by Maurice Hinson (Alfred, Los Angeles).

Although there's no reference to it in this book, I've loved Frank Conroy's *Body & Soul* (Houghton Mifflin, Dell), a novel about a young boy, growing up as a prodigy.

And *Piano & Keyboard* magazine is helpful and interesting (bimonthly; String Letter Press, San Anselmo, California).

7. Reverie
Träumerei

ⓐ The first edition has M.M. ♩ = 100. The Clara Schumann edition has ♩ = 80.

ⓑ The first edition has 🎵, meaning *con pedale*. The pedal indications in light print are from the Clara Schumann edition.